The Faith and Practice
of Al-Ghazali

THE FAITH AND PRACTICE OF AL-GHAZALI

By

W. MONTGOMERY WATT

B. LITT., PH.D.

*Senior Lecturer in Arabic University
of Edinburgh*

KITABBHAVAN

New Delhi-2 (India)

KITAB BHAVAN
Exporters and Importers
1784, Kalan Mahal, Darya Ganj,
New Delhi-110002 (India)

Phones : 3274686, 3277392-93
Fax : 91-11-3263383
Telex : 31-63106 ALI IN

ISBN 81-7151-223-2

First Published in India 1996

Published by :
Nusrat Ali Nasri for Kitab Bhavan
1784, Kalan Mahal, Darya Ganj,
New Delhi-110002 (India)

Printed in India at:
F.M. Offset Printers
Darya Ganj,
New Delhi (India)

GENERAL INTRODUCTION

AS A RESULT of two Wars that have devastated the World men and women everywhere feel a twofold need. We need a deeper understanding and appreciation of other peoples and their civilizations, especially their moral and spiritual achievements. And we need a wider vision of the Universe, a clearer insight into the fundamentals of ethics and religion. How ought men to behave ? How ought nations ? Does God exist ? What is his Nature ? How is He related to His creatton ? Especially, how can man approach Him ? In other words, there is a general desire to know what the greatest minds, whether of East or West, have thought and said about the Truth of God and of the beings who (as most of them hold) have sprung from Him, live by Him, and return to Him.

It is the object of this Series, which originated among a group of Oxford men and their friends, to place the chief ethical and religious masterpieces of the world, both Christian and non-Christian, within easy reach of the intelligent reader who is not necessarily an expert— the ex-Service man who is interested in the East, the undergraduate, the adult student, the intelligent public generally. The Series will contain books of three kinds : translations, reproductions of ideal and religious art, and background books showing the surroundings in which the literature and art arose and developed. These books overlap each other. Religious art, both in East and West, often illustrates a religious text, and in suitable cases the text and the pictures will be printed together to complete each other. The background books will often consist largely of translations. The volumes will be prepared by scholars of distinction, who will try to make them, not only scholarly, but intelligible and enjoyable. This Introduction represents the views of the General Editors as to the scope of the Series, but not necessarily the views of all contributors to it. The contents of the books will also be very varied—ethical and social, biographical, devotional, philosophic and mystical, whether in poetry, in pictures or in prose. There is a great wealth of material. Confucius lived in a time much like our own, when State was at war with State and the people suffering and disillusioned ; and the 'Classics' he preserved or inspired show the social virtues that may unite families, classes and State into one great family, in obedience to the Will of Heaven. Asoka and Akbar (both of them great patrons of art) ruled a vast Empire on the principles of religious faith. There are the moral anecdotes and moral maxims of the Jewish and Muslim writers of the Middle Ages. There are the beautiful tales of courage, love and fidelity in the Indian and Persian epics. Shakespeare's plays show that he thought the true relation between man and man is love. Here and there a volume will illustrate the unethical or less ethical man and difficulties that beset him.

Then there are the devotional and philosophic works. The lives and legends (legends often express religious truth with clarity and beauty) of the Buddha, of the parents of Mary, of Francis of Assisi, and the exquisite sculptures and paintings that illustrate them. Indian and Christian religious music, and the words of prayer and praise which the music intensifies. There are the prophets and apocalyptic writers, Zarathustrian and Hebrew ; the Greek philosophers, Christian thinkers— and the Greek, Latin, medieval and modern—whom they so deeply influenced. There is, too, the Hindu, Buddhist and Christian teaching expressed in such great monuments as the Indian temples, Barabudur (the

Chartres of Asia) and Ajanta, Chartres itself and the Sistine Chapel.

Finally, there are the mystics of feeling, and the mystical philosophers. In God-loving India the poets, musicians, sculptors and painters inspired by the spiritual worship of Krishna and Rama, as well as the philosophic mystics from the Upanishads onward. The two great Taoists Lao-tze and Chuang-tze and the Sung mystical painters in China, Rumi and other sufis in Islam, Plato and Plotinus, followed by 'Dionysius', Eckhart, St. John of the Cross and (in our view) Dante and other great mystics and mystical painters in many Christian lands.

Mankind is hungry, but the feast is there, though it is locked up and hidden away. It is the aim of this Series to put it within reach, so, that, like the heroes of Homer, we may stretch forth our hands to the good cheer laid before us.

No doubt the great religions differ in fundamental respects. But they are not nearly so far from one another as they seem. We think they are further off than they are largely because we so often misunderstand and misrepresent them. Those whose own religion is dogmatic have often been as ready to learn from other teachings as those who are liberals in religion. Above all, there is an enormous amount of common ground in the great religions, concerning, too, the most fundamental matters. There is frequent agreement on the Divine Nature ; God is the One, Self-subsisting Reality, knowing Himself, and therefore loving and rejoicing in Himself. Nature and finite spirits are in some way subordinate kinds of Being, or merely appearances of the Divine, the One. The three stages of the way of man's approach or return to God are in essence the same in Christian and non-Christian teaching: an

7

ethical stage, then one of knowledge and love, leading to the mystical union of the soul with God. Each stage will be illustrated in these volumes.

Something of all this may (it is hoped) be learnt from the books and pictures in this Series. Read and pondered with a desire to learn, they will help men and women to find 'fullness of life', and peoples to live together in greater understanding and harmony. To-day the earth is beautiful, but men are disillusioned and afraid. But there may come a day, perhaps not a distant day, when there will be a renaissance of man's spirit: when men will be innocent and happy amid the beauty of the world, or their eyes will be opened to see that egoism and strife are folly, that the universe is fundamentally spiritual, and that men are the sons of God.

> They shall not hurt nor destroy
> In all My holy mountain:
> For all the earth shall be full of the
>   knowledge of the Lord
> As the waters cover the sea.

THE EDITORS

I should like to record my thanks to Professors H. A. R. Gibb and A. J. Arberry for various forms of help and encouragement. To my colleague, Dr. Pierre Cachia, I am particularly indebted for the compilation of the Index and for advice on some points of detail. For those unfamiliar with Arabic terms the Index may serve to some extent as a glossary. The quotations from the Qur'an (for which the abbreviation ' Q.' is used) are taken from the late Richard Bell's translation (Edinburgh, 1937-9), but have occasionally been modified to suit the context. In Appendix A (3) of my article, 'The authenticity of Works attributed to al-Ghazālī,' in the *Journal of the Royal Asiatic Society* for 1952 I have attempted to show that the closing section of *The Beginning of Guidance* (omitted from the translation below) is spurious.

W. Montgomery Watt

The University,
 Edinburgh.
  May 1952.

9

INTRODUCTION

Abū Ḥāmid Muḥammad al-Ghazālī was born at Ṭūs in Persia in 450 A.H. (1058 A.D.). His father died when he was quite young, but the guardian saw to it that this 'lad o' pairts' and his brother received a good education. After the young Ghazālī had spent some years of study under the greatest theologian of the age, al-Juwaynī, Imām al-Ḥaramayn, his outstanding intellectual gifts were noted by Niẓām al-Mulk, the all-powerful vizier of the Turkish sultan who ruled the 'Abbasid caliphate of Baghdad, and he appointed him professor at the university he had founded in the capital. Thus at the age of thirty-three he had attained to one of the most distinguished positions in the academic world of his day.

Four years later, however, he had to meet a crisis; it had physical symptoms but it was primarily religious. He came to feel that the one thing that mattered was avoidance of Hell and attainment of Paradise, and he saw that his present way of life was too worldly to have any hope of eternal reward. After a severe inner struggle he left Baghdad to take up the life of a wandering ascetic. Though later he returned to the task of teaching, the change that occurred in him at this crisis was permanent. He was now a religious man, not just a worldly teacher of religious sciences. He died at Ṭūs in 505 (1111).

The first of the books here translated, *Deliverance from Error* (literally, 'What delivers from error'—*al-Munqidh min-aḍ-Ḍalāl*), is the source for much of what we know about al-Ghazālī's life. It is autobiographical, yet not exactly an autobiography. It presents us with an intellectual analysis of his spiritual growth, and also

11

offers arguments in defence of the view that there is a form of human apprehension higher than rational apprehension, namely, that of the prophet when God reveals truths to him. Moreover close study shows that al-Ghazālī does not always observe strict chronology, but has schematized his description of his intellectual development. Al-Ghazālī introduces his discussions in a manner reminiscent of Descartes. The 'bonds of mere authority' ceased to hold him, as they ceased to hold the father of modern European philosophy. Looking for 'necessary' truths al-Ghazālī came, like Descartes, to doubt the infallibility of sense-perception, and to rest his philosophy rather on principles which are intuitively certain. With this in mind al-Ghazālī divided the various 'seekers' after truth into the four distinct groups of Theologians, Philosophers, Authoritarians and Mystics.

(1) Scholastic theology had already achieved a fair degree of elaboration in the defence of Islamic orthodoxy, as a perusal of *al-Irshād* by al-Juwaynī, (translated into French), will show. Al-Ghazālī had been brought up in this tradition, and did not cease to be a theologian when he became a mystic. His criticism of the theologians is mild. He regards contemporary theology as successful in attaining its aims, but inadequate to meet his own special needs because it did not go far enough in the elucidation of its assumptions. There was no radical change in his theological views when he became a mystic, only a change in his interests, and some of his earlier works in the field of dogmatics are quoted with approval in *al-Munqidh*.

(2) The Philosophers with whom al-Ghazālī was chiefly concerned were those he calls 'theistic', above all, al-Fārābi and Ibn Sīnā (Avicenna). Their philo-

sophy was a form of Neoplatonism, sufficiently adapted to Islamic monotheism for them to claim to be Muslims. Though the part they played in stimulating the medieval Christian scholastics is acknowledged, the contribution of these men to the intellectual progress of mankind as a whole has not yet been fully appreciated. To the great body of Muslims, however, some of their positions were unacceptable, because they tended to contradict principles essential to the daily life of believing Muslims. The achievement of al-Ghazālī was to master their technique of thinking—mainly Aristotelian logic—and then, making use of that, to refashion the basis of Islamic theology, to incorporate as much of the Neoplatonists' teaching as was compatible with Islam, and to expose the logical weakness of the rest of their philosophy. The fusion of Greek philosophical techniques with Islamic dogma which had been partly accomplished by al-Ash'arī (d. 324/935) was thus in essence completed, though the working-out was left to al Ghazālī's successors. Undoubtedly al-Ghazālī learnt much from these Neoplatonists, but the allegations that he finally adopted some of their fundamental principles, which he had earlier criticized, are to be denied, since they are based on works falsely attributed to al-Ghazālī.

(3) Those whom al-Ghazālī calls the party of *ta'līm* or 'authoritative instruction' (also known as Ismā'īlīyah and Bāṭinīyah) held that truth is to be attained not by reason but by accepting the pronouncement of the infallible Imām. The doctrine had an important political reference since it was the official ideology of a rival state, the Fāṭimid caliphate with centre in Cairo, and thus anyone who held it was suspect of being, at the least, a 'fellow-traveller'.

(4) There had been an ascetic element in Islam from the time of Muḥammad himself, and this could easily be

13

combined with orthodoxy. Ṣufism, however, was usually something more than asceticism, and the strictly mystical elements which it contained often led to heterodox theology. From the Ṣūfīs or mystics al-Ghazālī received more help with his personal problems, yet he could also criticize their extravagances, like the words of al-Ḥallāj, 'I am the Ultimate Reality'. Al-Ghazālī was at great pains to keep his mysticism in harmony with orthodox dogma and with the performance of the common religious duties. When he became a mystic he did not cease to be a good Muslim any more than he ceased to be an Ash'arite theologian.

What al-Ghazālī learn in the years of solitude after he left Baghdad he tried to set down in his greatest work, *The Revival of the Religious Sciences (Iḥyā' 'Ulūm ad-Dīn)*. The second of the books translated below, *The Beginning of Guidance (Bidāyat al Hidāyah)*, presents one side of the teaching there given, namely, the religious practices and the conduct in social relationships which al-Ghazālī set up as an ideal. Thus *The Beginning of Guidance* is an introduction to the *Iḥyā'*; it deals with the 'purgative way' and directs the reader to the larger work for what lies beyond that. The ideal resembles that of a monastic third order with a *very* strict rule; it does not seem to be suited to the hurried life of a modern city. Yet al-Ghazālī's seriousness and sense of urgency stand out vividly and communicate themselves. The book is interesting, too, in that, though al-Ghazālī's standpoint is almost modern in many ways, dark forces of superstition are prominent in the background.

Al-Ghazālī has sometimes been acclaimed in both East and West as the greatest Muslim after Muḥammad and he is by no means unworthy of that dignity. His greatness rests above all on two things: (1) He was the leader in Islam's supreme encounter with Greek

14

philosophy—that encounter from which Islamic theology emerged victorious and enriched, and in which Arabic Neoplatonism received a blow from which it did not recover. (2) He brought orthodoxy and mysticism into closer contact; the orthodox theologians still went their own way, and so did the mystics, but the theologians became more ready to accept the mystics as respectable, while the mystics were more careful to remain within the bounds of orthodoxy.

Yet perhaps the greatest thing about al-Ghazālī was his personality, and it may yet again be a source of inspiration. Islam is now wrestling with Western thought as it once wrestled with Greek philosophy, and is as much in need as it was then of a 'revival of the religious sciences'. Deep study of al-Ghazālī may suggest to Muslims steps to be taken if they are to deal successfully with the contemporary situation. Christians, too, now that the world is in a cultural melting-pot, must be prepared to learn from Islam, and are unlikely to find a more sympathetic guide than al-Ghazālī.

NOTES ON THE TRANSLATION.

The word *Salāt* has been rendered 'Worship' rather than 'prayers, following Professor Calverley, *Worship in Islam*, since it seemed desirable to keep 'prayer' for *duʿāʾ*. For an explanation of the technical terms connected with the Worship see the above volume, or *Encyclopedia of Islam*, art. *Ṣalāt*, or Hughes, *Dictionary of Islam*, art. *Prayer*.

The text of *al-Munqidh* used was that of the third Damascus edition of Jamīl Salība and Kāmil ʿAyyād, dated 1358/1939; that of the *Bidāyah* one dated Cairo 1353/1934. I have deviated from the printed text of *al-Munqidh* at the following points: p. 99, line 6, *awliyāʾ* instead of *anbiyāʾ*; p. 125, 6, omit semicolon and vocalize as *ʿilma-hu*; 143, 3 vocalize as *turaddu* instead of *taridu*. In the *Bidāyah*, 39, 14 add *li* or *ma* before *yastaʿin*. (=translation p. 151).

CONTENTS

DELIVERANCE FROM ERROR

AND ATTACHMENT TO THE LORD OF MIGHT AND MAJESTY

In the name of God, the Merciful and Compassionate

I. INTRODUCTION

Praise be to Him with Whose praise every message and every discourse commences. And blessings be upon Muhammad the Chosen, the Prophet and Messenger, and on his house and his Companions, who guide men away from error.

You have asked me, my brother in religion, to show you the aims and inmost nature of the sciences and the perplexing depths of the religious systems. You have begged me to relate to you the difficulties I encountered in my attempt to extricate the truth from the confusion of contending sects and to distinguish the different ways and methods, and the venture I made in climbing from the plain of naive and second-hand belief (*taqlīd*) to the peak of direct vision. You want me to describe, firstly what profit I derived from the science of theology (*kalam*), secondly, what I disapprove of in the methods of the party of *ta'līm* (authoritative instruction), who **66** restrict the apprehension of truth to the blind following (*taqlīd*) of the Imam, thirdly, what I rejected of the methods of philosophy, and lastly, what I approved in the Sufi way of life. You would know, too, what essential truths became clear to me in my manifold investigations into the doctrines held by men, why I gave up teaching in Baghdad although I had many students, and why I returned to it at Naysābūr (Nīshāpūr) after a long interval. I am proceeding to answer your request, for I recognise that your desire is genuine. In this I seek the help of God and trust in Him ; I ask His succour and take refuge with Him.

You must know—and may God most high perfect you in the right way and soften your hearts to receive the truth—that the different religious observances and religious communities of the human race and likewise the different theological systems of the religious leaders, with all the multiplicity of sects and variety of practices, 67 constitute ocean depths in which the majority drown and only a minority reach safety. Each separate group thinks that it alone is saved, and 'each party is rejoicing in what they have' (Q. 32, 55 ; 30, 31). This is what was foretold by the prince of the Messengers (God bless him), who is true and trustworthy, when he said, 'My community will be split up into seventy-three sects, and but one of them is saved' ; and what he foretold has indeed almost come about.

From my early youth, since I attained the age of puberty before I was twenty, until the present time when I am over fifty, I have ever recklessly launched out into the midst of these ocean depths, I have ever bravely embarked on this open sea, throwing aside all craven caution ; I have poked into every dark recess, I have made an assault on every problem, I have plunged into every abyss, I have scrutinized the creed of every sect, I have tried to lay bare the inmost doctrines of every community. All this have I done that I might 68 distinguish between true and false, between sound tradition and heretical innovation. Whenever I meet one of the Bāṭinīyah, I like to study his creed ; whenever I meet one of the Zāhirīyah, I want to know the essentials of his belief. If it is a philosopher, I try to become acquainted with the essence of his philosophy ; if a scholastic theologian I busy myself in examining his theological reasoning ; if a Sufi, I yearn to fathom the secret of his mysticism ; if an ascetic (*muta'abbid*), I investigate the basis of his ascetic practices ; if one of the Zanādiqah or Mu'aṭṭilah, I look beneath the surface **69** to discover the reasons for his bold adoption of such a creed.

To thirst after a comprehension of things as they really are was my habit and custom from a very early age. It was instinctive with me, a part of my God-given nature, a matter of temperament and not of my choice or contriving. Consequently as I drew near the age of adolescence the bonds of mere authority (*taqlid*) ceased to hold me and inherited beliefs lost their grip upon me, for I saw that Christian youths always grew up to be Christians, Jewish youths to be Jews and Muslim youths to be Muslims. I heard, too, the **70** Tradition related of the Prophet of God according to which he said : 'Everyone who is born is born with a sound nature ;[1] it is his parents who make him a Jew or a Christian or a Magian.' My inmost being was moved to discover what his original nature really was and what the beliefs derived from the authority of parents and teachers really were. The attempt to distinguish between these authority-based opinions and their principles developed the mind, for in distinguishing the true in them from the false differences appeared.

I therefore said within myself : 'To begin with, what I am looking for is knowledge of what things really are, so I must undoubtedly try to find what knowledge really is'. It was plain to me that sure and certain knowledge is that knowledge in which the object is disclosed in such a fashion that no doubt remains along

---

[1] The interpretation of this tradition has been much discussed; cp. art. Fitra by D. B. Macdonald in EI. The above meaning appears to be that adopted by al-Ghazālī.

with it, that no possibility of error or illusion accompanies it, and that the mind cannot even entertain such a supposition. Certain knowledge must also be infallible ; and this infallibility or security from error is such that no attempt to show the falsity of the knowledge can occasion doubt or denial, even though the attempt is made by someone who turns stones into gold or a rod into a serpent. Thus, I know that ten is more than three. Let us suppose that someone says to me : 'No, three is more than ten, and in proof of that I shall change this rod into a serpent' ; and let us suppose that he actually changes the rod into a serpent and that I witness him doing so. No doubts about what I know are raised in me because of this. The only result is that I wonder precisely how he is able to produce this change. Of doubt about my knowledge there is no trace.

After these reflections I knew that whatever I do not know in this fashion and with this mode of certainty is not reliable and infallible knowledge ; and knowledge that is not infallible is not certain knowledge.

II.   PRELIMINARIES :

SCEPTICISM AND THE DENIAL OF ALL KNOWLEDGE

Thereupon I investigated the various kinds of knowledge I had, and found myself destitute of all knowledge with this characteristic of infallibility except in the case of sense-perception and necessary truths. So I said : 'Now that despair has come over me, there is no point in studying any problems except on the basis of what is self-evident, namely, necessary truths and the affirmations of the senses, I must first bring these to be judged in order that I may be certain on this matter. Is my reliance on sense-perception and my trust in the soundness of necessary truths of the same kind as my previous trust in the beliefs I had merely taken over from others and as the trust most men have in the results of thinking ? Or is it a justified trust that is in no danger of being betrayed or destroyed'?

I proceeded therefore with extreme earnestness to 73 reflect on sense-perception and on necessary truths, to see whether I could make myself doubt them. The outcome of this protracted effort to induce doubt was that I could no longer trust sense-perception either. Doubt began to spread here and say : 'From where does this reliance on sense-perception come ? The most powerful sense is that of sight. Yet when it looks at the shadow (*sc.* of a stick or the gnomon of a sundial), it sees it standing still, and judges that there is no motion. Then by experiment and observation after an hour it knows that shadow is moving and, moreover, that it is moving not by fits and starts but gradually and steadily by infinitely small distances in such a way that it is never in a state of rest. Again, it looks at the heavenly body (*sc.* the sun) and sees it small, the size of a shilling;[1] yet geometrical computations show that it is greater than the earth in size'.

In this and similar cases of sense-perception the sense as judge forms his judgements, but another judge, the intellect, shows him repeatedly to be wrong ; and the charge of falsity cannot be rebutted.

To this I said : 'My reliance on sense-perception also has been destroyed. Perhaps only those intellectual truths which are first principles (or derived from first principles) are to be relied upon, such as the assertion that ten are more than three, that the same thing cannot be both affirmed and denied at one time, that one thing is 74 not both generated in time and eternal, nor both existent and non-existent, nor both nece.sary and impossible'.

[1] Literally *dinār.*

23

Sense-perception replied : 'Do you not expect that your reliance on intellectual truths will fare like your reliance on sense-perception? You used to trust in me; then along came the intellect-judge and proved me wrong ; if it were not for the intellect-judge you would have continued to regard me as true. Perhaps behind intellectual apprehension there is another judge who, if he manifests himself, will show the falsity of intellect in its judging, just as, when intellect manifested itself, it showed the falsity of sense in its judging. The fact that such a supra-intellectual apprehension has not manifested itself is no proof that it is impossible'.

My ego hesitated a little about the reply to that, and sense-perception heightened the difficulty by referring to dreams. 'Do you not see', it said, 'how, when you are asleep, you believe things and imagine circumstances, holding them to be stable and enduring, and, so long as you are in that dream-condition, have no doubts about them ? And is it not the case that when you awake you know that all you have imagined and believed is unfounded and ineffectual? Why then are you confident that all your waking beliefs, whether from sense or intellect, are genuine ? They are true in respect of your present state ; but it is possible that a state will come upon you whose relation to your waking consciousness is analogous to the relation of the latter to dreaming. In comparison with this state your waking consciousness would be like dreaming ! When you have entered into this state, you will be certain that all the suppositions of your intellect are empty imaginings. It may be that
75 that state is what the Sufis claim as their special 'state' (*sc.* mystic union or ecstasy), for they consider that in their 'states' (or ecstasies), which occur when they have withdrawn into themselves and are absent from their senses, they witness states (or circumstances) which do

24

not tally with these principles of the intellect. Perhaps that 'state' is death; for the Messenger of God (God bless and preserve him) says: 'The people are dreaming; when they die, they become awake.' So perhaps life in this world is a dream by comparison with the world to come; and when a man dies, things come to appear differently to him from what he now beholds, and at the same time the words are addressed to him: 'We have taken off thee thy covering, and thy sight tody is sharp' (Q. 50, 21).

When these thoughts had occurred to me and penetrated my being, I tried to find some way of treating my unhealthy condition; but it was not easy. Such ideas can only be repelled by demonstration; but a demonstration requires a knowledge of first principles; since this is not admitted, however, it is impossible to make the demonstration. The disease was baffling, and lasted almost two months, during which I was a sceptic in fact though not in theory nor in outward expression. At length God cured me of the malady; my being was restored to health and an even balance; the necessary truths of the intellect became once more accepted, as I regained confidence in their certain and trustworthy character.

This did not come about by systematic demonstration or marshalled argument, but by a light which God most high cast into my breast. That light is the key to the greater part of knowledge. Whoever thinks that the understanding of things Divine rests upon strict proofs has in his thought narrowed down the wideness of God's mercy. When the Messenger of God (peace be upon him) was asked about 'enlarging' (sharḥ) and its meaning in the verse, 'Whenever God wills to guide a man, He enlarges his breast for islām (i.e., surrender to God)' (Q. 6, 125), he said, 'It is a light which God most

25

high casts into the heart'. When asked, 'What is the sign of it ?', he said, 'Withdrawal from the mansion of deception and return to the mansion of eternity.' It was about this light that Muhammad (peace be upon him) said, 'God created the creatures in darkness, and then sprinkled upon them some of His light.' From that light must be sought an intuitive understanding of things Divine. That light at certain times gushes from the spring of Divine generosity, and for it one must watch and wait—as Muhammad (peace be upon him) said : 'In the days of your age your Lord has gusts of favour ; then place yourselves in the way of them'.

The point of these accounts is that the task is perfectly fulfilled when the quest is prosecuted up to the stage of seeking what is not sought (but stops short of that). For first principles are not sought, since they are present and to hand ; and if what is present is sought for, it becomes hidden and lost. When, however, a man seeks what is sought (and that only), he is not accused of falling short in the seeking of what is sought.

III. THE CLASSES OF SEEKERS

When God by His grace and abundant generosity cured me of this disease, I came to regard the various seekers (sc. after truth) as comprising four groups :—

(1) the *Theologians* (*mutakallimūn*), who claim that they are the exponents of thought and intellectual speculation;

(2) the *Bāṭinīyah*, who consider that they, as the party of 'authoritative instruction' (*ta'līm*), alone derive truth from the infallible *imam*;

(3) the *Philosophers*, who regard themselves as the exponents of logic and demonstration;

(4) the *Sufis* or *Mystics* who claim that they alone

enter into the 'presence' (*sc.* of God), and possess vision and intuitive understanding.

I said within myself: 'The truth cannot lie outside these four classes. These are the people who tread the paths of the quest for truth. If the truth is not with them, no point remains in trying to apprehend the truth. There is certainly no point in trying to return to the level of naive and derivative belief (*taqlīd*) once it has been left, since a condition of being at such a level is that one should not know one is there; when a man comes to know that, the glass of his naive beliefs is broken. This is a breakage which cannot be mended, a breakage not to be repaired by patching or by assembling of fragments. The glass must be melted once again in the furnace for a new start, and out of it another fresh vessel formed'.

I now hastened to follow out these four ways and investigate what these groups had achieved, commencing with the science of theology and then taking the way of philosophy, the 'authoritative instruction' of the Bāṭinīyah, and the way of mysticism, in that order.

1. *The Science of Theology : its Aims and Achievements.* 80

I commenced, then, with the science of Theology ('*ilm al-kalām*), and obtained a thorough grasp of it. I read the books of sound theologians and myself wrote some books on the subject. But it was a science, I found, 81 which, though attaining its own aim, did not attain mine. Its aim was merely to preserve the creed of orthodoxy and to defend it against the deviations of heretics.

Now God sent to His servants by the mouth of His messenger, in the Qur'an and Traditions, a creed which is the truth and whose contents are the basis of man's welfare in both religious and secular affairs. But Satan

27

too sent, in the suggestions of heretics, things contrary to orthodoxy; men tended to accept his suggestions and almost corrupted the true creed for its adherents. So God brought into being the class of theologians, and moved them to support traditional orthodoxy with the weapon of systematic argument by laying bare the confused doctrines invented by the heretics at variance with traditional orthodoxy. This is the origin of theology and theologians.

In due course a group of theologians performed the task to which God invited them; they successfully preserved orthodoxy, defended the creed received from the prophetic source and rectified heretical innovations. Nevertheless in so doing they based their arguments on premisses which they took from their opponents and which they were compelled to admit by naive belief (*taqlīd*), or the consensus of the community, or bare acceptance of Qur'an and Traditions. For the most part their efforts were devoted to making explicit the contradictions of their opponents and criticizing them in respect of the logical consequences of what they admitted.

This was of little use in the case of one who admitted nothing at all save logically necessary truths. Theology was not adequate to my case and was unable to cure the malady of which I complained. It is true that, when theology appeared as a recognized discipline and much effort had been expended in it over a considerable period of time, the theologians, becoming very earnest in their endeavours to defend orthodoxy by the study of what things really are, embarked on a study of substances and accidents with their nature and properties. But, since that was not the aim of their science, they did not deal with the question thoroughly in their thinking and consequently did not arrive at results sufficient to

28

dispel universally the darkness of confusion due to the different views of men. I do not exclude the possibility that for others than myself these results have been sufficient; indeed, I do not doubt that this has been so for quite a number. But these results were mingled with naive belief in certain matters which are not included among first principles.

My purpose here, however, is to describe my own case, not to disparage those who sought a remedy thereby, for the healing drugs vary with the disease. How often one sick man's medicine proves to be another's poison!

2. *Philosophy.*

After I had done with theology I started on philosophy. I was convinced that a man cannot grasp what is defective in any of the sciences unless he has so complete a grasp of the science in question that he equals its most learned exponents in the appreciation of its fundamental principles, and even goes beyond and surpasses them, probing into some of the tangles and profundities which the very professors of the science have neglected. Then and only then is it possible that what he has to assert about its defects is true. 84

So far as I could see none of the doctors of Islam had devoted thought and attention to philosophy. In their writings none of the theologians engaged in polemic against the philosophers, apart from obscure and scattered utterances so plainly erroneous and inconsistent that no person of ordinary intelligence would be likely to be deceived, far less one versed in the sciences.

I realized that to refute a system before understanding it and becoming acquainted with its depths is to act blindly. I therefore set out in all earnestness to acquire 85

29

a knowledge of philosophy from books, by private study without the help of an instructor. I made progress towards this aim during my hours of free time after teaching in the religious sciences and writing, for at this period I was burdened with the teaching and instruction of three hundred students in Baghdad. By my solitary reading during the hours thus snatched God brought me in less than two years to a complete understanding of the sciences of the philosophers. Thereafter I continued to reflect assiduously for nearly a year on what I had assimilated, going over it in my mind again and again and probing its tangled depths, until I comprehended surely and certainly how far it was deceitful and confusing and how far true and a representation of reality.

Hear now an account of this discipline and of the achievement of the sciences it comprises. There are various schools of philosophers, I perceived, and their sciences are divided into various branches ; but throughout their numerous schools they suffer from the defect of being infidels and irreligious men, even although of the different groups of philosophers—older and most ancient, earlier and more recent—some are much closer to the truth than others.

86 A. *The schools of philosophers, and how the defect of unbelief affects them all.* The many philosophical sects and systems constitute three main groups : the Materialists (*Dahrīyūn*), the Naturalists (*Tabī'īyūn*), and the Theists (*Ilāhīyūn*).

The first group, the *Materialists*, are among the earliest philosophers. They deny the Creator and Disposer of the world, omniscient and omnipotent, and consider that the world has everlastingly existed just as it is, of itself and without a creator, and that everlastingly animals have come from seed and seed from animals ; thus it was and thus it ever will be. These are the Zanādiqah or irreligious people.

The second group, the *Naturalists,* are a body of philosophers who have engaged in manifold researches into the world of nature and the marvels of animals and plants and have expended much effort in the science of dissecting the organs of animals. They see there sufficient of the wonders of God's creation and the inventions of His wisdom to compel them to acknowledge a 87 wise Creator Who is aware of the aims and purposes of things. No one can make a careful study of anatomy and the wonderful uses of the members and organs without attaining to the necessary knowledge that there is a perfection in the order which the framer gave to the animal frame, and especially to that of man.

Yet these philosophers, immersed in their researches into nature, take the view that the equal balance of the temperament has great influence in constituting the powers of animals. They hold that even the intellectual power in man is dependent on the temperament, so that as the temperament is corrupted intellect also is corrupted and ceases to exist. Further, when a thing ceases to exist, it is unthinkable in their opinion that the non-existent should return to existence. Thus it is their views that the soul dies and does not return to life, and they deny the future life—heaven, hell, resurrection and judgement ; there does not remain, they hold, any reward for obedience or any punishment for sin. With the curb removed they give way to a bestial indulgence of their appetites.

These are also irreligious for the basis of faith is faith in God and in the Last Day, and these, though believing in God and His attributes, deny the Last Day.

The third group, the *Theists,* are the more modern

31

philosophers and include Socrates, his pupil Plato, and
88 the latter's pupil Aristotle. It was Aristotle who
systematized logic for them and organized the sciences,
securing a higher degree of accuracy and bringing
them to maturity.

The Theists in general attacked the two previous
groups, the Materialists and the Naturalists, and exposed their defects so effectively that others were
relieved of the task. 'And God relieved the believers of
fighting' (Q. 33, 25) through their mutual combat.
Aristotle, moreover, attacked his predecessors among
the Theistic philosophers, especially Plato and Socrates,
and went so far in his criticisms that he separated himself from them all. Yet he too retained a residue of their
unbelief and heresy from which he did not manage to
free himself. We must therefore reckon as unbelievers
both these philosophers themselves and their followers
among the Islamic philosophers, such as Ibn Sīna, al-
89 Fārābī and others; in transmitting the philosophy of
Aristotle, however, none of the Islamic philosophers has
accomplished anything comparable to the achievements
of the two men named. The translations of others are
marked by disorder and confusion, which so perplex the
understanding of the student that he fails to compre-
hend; and if a thing is not comprehended how can it be
either refuted or accepted?

All that, in our view, genuinely is part of the philosophy of Aristotle, as these men have transmitted it,
falls under three heads: (1) what must be counted as
unbelief; (2) what must be counted as heresy; (3) what
is not to be denied at all. Let us proceed, then, to the
details.

90 B. *The Various Philosophical Sciences*. For our present
purpose the philosophical sciences are six in number:

32

mathematics, logic, natural science, theology, politics, ethics.

1. MATHEMATICS. This embraces arithmetic, plane geometry and solid geometry. None of its results are connected with religious matters, either to deny or to affirm them. They are matters of demonstration which it is impossible to deny once they have been understood and apprehended. Nevertheless there are two draw-backs which arise from mathematics.

(a) The first is that every student of mathematics admires its precision and the clarity of its demonstrations. This leads him to believe in the philosophers and to think that all their sciences resemble this one in clarity and demonstrative cogency. Further, he has already heard the accounts on everyone's lips of their unbelief, their denial of God's attributes, and their contempt for revealed truth ; he becomes an unbeliever merely by accepting them as authorities (*bi'l-taqlīd al-mahḍ*), and says to himself, 'If religion were true, it would not have escaped the notice of these men since they are so precise in this science'. Thus, after becoming acquainted by hearsay with their unbelief and denial of religion, he draws the conclusion that the truth is the denial and rejection of religion. How many have I seen who err from the truth because of this high opinion of the philosophers and without any other basis !

Against them one may argue : 'The man who excels in one art does not necessarily excel in every art. It is not necessary that the man who excels in law and theology should excel in medicine, nor that the man who is ignorant of intellectual speculations should be igno-rant of grammar. Rather, every art has people who have obtained excellence and preeminence in it, even though stupidity and ignorance may characterize them in other arts. The arguments in elementary matters of mathematics are demonstrative whereas those in theology (or metaphysics) are based on conjecture. This point is familiar only to those who have studied the matter deeply for themselves'.

If such a person is fixed in this belief which he has chosen out of respect for authority (taqlīd), he is not moved by this argument but is carried by strength of passion, love of vanity and the desire to be thought clever to persist in his good opinion of the philosophers with regard to all the sciences.

This is a great drawback, and because of it those who devote themselves eagerly to the mathematical sciences ought to be restrained. Even if their subject-matter is not relevant to religion, yet, since they belong to the foundations of the philosophical sciences, the student is infected with the evil and corruption of the philosophers. Few there are who devote themselves to this study without being stripped of religion and having the bridle of godly fear removed from their heads.

92 (b) The second drawback arises from the man who is loyal to Islam but ignorant. He thinks that religion must be defended by rejecting every science connected with the philosophers, and so rejects all their sciences and accuses them of ignorance therein. He even rejects their theory of the eclipse of sun and moon, considering that what they say is contrary to revelation. When that view is thus attacked, someone hears who has knowledge of such matters by apodeictic demonstration. He does not doubt his demonstration, but, believing that Islam is based on ignorance and the denial of apodeictic proof, grows in love for philosophy and hatred for Islam.

A grievous crime indeed against religion has been committed by the man who imagines that Islam is defended by the denial of the mathematical sciences, seeing that there is nothing in revealed truth opposed to these sciences by way of either negation or affirmation, and nothing in these sciences opposed to the truths of religion. Muhammad (peace be upon him) said, 'The sun and the moon are two of the signs of God; they are not eclipsed for anyone's death nor for his life; if you see such an event, take refuge in the recollection of God (most high) and in prayer'. There is nothing here 93 obliging us to deny the science of arithmetic which informs us specifically of the orbits of sun and moon, and their conjunction and opposition. (The further saying of Muhammad (peace be upon him), 'When God manifests Himself to a thing, it submits to him', is an addition which does not occur at all in the collections of sound Traditions.)

This is the character of mathematics and its drawbacks.

2. LOGIC. Nothing in logic is relevant to religion by way of denial or affirmation. Logic is the study of the methods of demonstration and of forming syllogisms, of the conditions for the premises of proofs, of the manner of combining the premises, of the conditions for sound definition and the manner of ordering it. Knowledge comprises (a) the concept (*taṣawwur*), which is apprehended by definition, and (b) the assertion or judgement (*taṣdīq*), which is apprehended by proof. There is 94 nothing here which requires to be denied. Matters of this kind are actually mentioned by the theologians and speculative thinkers in connection with the topic of demonstrations. The philosophers differ from these only in the expressions and technical terms they employ and in their greater elaboration of the explanations and classifications. An example of this is their proposition, 'If it is true that all A is B, then it follows that some B is A', that is, 'If it is true that all men are animals, then it

follows that some animals are men'. They express this by saying that 'the universal affirmative proposition has as its converse a particular affirmative proposition'. What connection has this with the essentials of religion, that it should be denied or rejected ? If such a denial is made, the only effect upon the logicians is to impair their belief in the intelligence of the man who made the denial and, what is worse, in his religion, inasmuch as he considers that it rests on such denials.

Moreover, there is a type of mistake into which students of logic are liable to fall. They draw up a list of the conditions to be fulfilled by demonstration, which are known without fail to produce certainty. When, however, they come at length to treat of religious questions, not merely are they unable to satisfy these conditions, but they admit an extreme degree of relaxation (*sc.* of their standards of proof). Frequently, too, the student who admires logic and sees its clarity, imagines that the infidel doctrines attributed to the phi' phers are supported by similar demonstrations, a d hastens into unbelief before reaching the theological (or metaphysical) sciences. Thus this drawback too leads to unbelief.

3. NATURAL SCIENCE OR PHYSICS. This is the investigation of the sphere of the heavens together with the heavenly bodies, and of what is beneath the heavens, both simple bodies like water, air, earth, fire, and composite bodies like animals, plants and minerals, and also of the causes of their changes, transformations and combinations. This is similar to the investigation by medicine of the human body with its principal and subordinate organs, and of the causes of the changes of temperament. Just as it is not a condition of religion to reject medical science, so likewise the rejection of natural science is not one of its conditions, except with

regard to particular points which I enumerate in my book, *The Incoherence of the Philosophers*. Any other points on which a different view has to be taken from the philosophers · are shown by reflection to be implied in those mentioned. The basis of all these objections is the recognition that nature is in subjection to God most high, not acting of itself but serving as an instrument in the hands of its Creator. Sun and moon, stars and elements, are in subjection to His command. There is none of them whose activity is produced by or proceeds from its own essence.

4. THEOLOGY OR METAPHYSICS. Here occur most of the errors of the philosophers. They are unable to satisfy the conditions of proof they lay down in logic, and consequently differ much from one another here. The views of Aristotle, as expounded by al-Fārābī and Ibn Sīna, are close to those of the Islamic writers. All their errors are comprised under twenty heads, on three of which they must be reckoned infidels and on seventeen heretics. It was to show the falsity of their views on these twenty points that I composed *The Incoherence of the Philosophers*. The three points in which they differ from all the Muslims are as follows :

(a) They say that for bodies there is no resurrection; it is bare spirits which are rewarded or punished ; and the rewards and punishments are spiritual, not bodily. They certainly speak truth in affirming the spiritual ones, since these do exist as well ; but they speak falsely in denying the bodily ones and in their pronouncements disbelieve the Divine law.

(b) They say that God knows universals but not particulars. This too is plain unbelief. The truth is that 'there does not escape Him the weight of an atom in the heavens or in the earth' (Q. 34, 3).

(c) They say that the world is everlasting, without

beginning or end. But no Muslim has adopted any such view on this question.

On the further points—their denial of the attributes of God, their doctrine that God knows by His essence and not by a knowledge which is over and above His essence, and the like—their position approximates to that of the Mu'tazilah ; and the Mu'tazilah must not be accounted infidels because of such matters. In my book, *The Decisive Criterion for distinguishing Islam from Heresy*, I have presented the grounds for regarding as corrupt the opinion of those who hastily pronounce a man an infidel if he deviates from their own system of doctrine.

5. P O L I T I C S. All their discussion of this is based on considerations of worldly and governmental advantage. These they borrow from the Divine scriptures revealed through the prophets and from the maxims handed down from the saints of old.

6. E T H I C S. Their whole discussion of ethics consists in defining the characteristic and moral constitution of the soul and enumerating the various types of soul and the method of moderating and controlling them. This they borrow from the teaching of the mystics, those men of piety whose chief occupation is to meditate upon God, to oppose the passions, and to walk in the way leading to God by withdrawing from worldly pleasure. In their spiritual warfare they have learnt about the virtues and vices of the soul and the defects in its actions, and what they have learned they have clearly expressed. The philosophers have taken over this teaching and mingled it with their own disquisitions, furtively using the embellishment to sell their rubbishy wares more readily. Assuredly there was in the age of the philosophers, as indeed there is in every age, a group of those godly men, of whom God never denudes the world. They are the pillars of the earth, and by

their blessings mercy comes down on the people of the earth, as we read in the Tradition where Muhammad (peace be upon him) says : 'Through them you receive rain, through them you receive sustenance ; of their number were the men of the Cave'. And these, as the Qur'an declares, existed in early times (cp. Surah 18).

From this practice of the philosophers of incorporating in their books conceptions drawn from the prophets and mystics, their arise two evil tendencies, one in their partisans and one in their opponents.

(a) The evil tendency in the case of the opponent is serious. A crowd of men of slight intellect imagines that, since those ethical conceptions occur in the books of the philosophers mixed with their own rubbish, all reference to them must be avoided, and indeed any person mentioning them must be considered a liar. They imagine this because they heard of the conceptions in the first place only from the philosophers, and their weak intellects have concluded that, since their author is a falsifier, they must be false.

This is like a man who hears a Christian assert, 'There is no god but God, and Jesus is the Messenger of God'. The man rejects this, saying, 'This is a Christian conception', and does not pause to ask himself whether the Christian is an infidel in respect of this assertion or in respect of his denial of the prophethood of Muhammad (peace be upon him). If he is an infidel only in respect of his denial of Muhammad, then he need not be contradicted in other assertions, true in themselves and not connected with his unbelief, even though these are also true in his eyes.

It is customary with weaker intellects thus to take the men as criterion of the truth and not the truth as criterion of the men. The intelligent men follows 'Alī (may God be pleased with him) when he said, 'Do not

39

know the truth by the men, but know the truth, and then you will know who are truthful'. The intelligent man knows the truth ; then he examines the particular assertion. If it is true, he accepts it, whether the speaker is a truthful person or not. Indeed he is often anxious to separate out the truth from the discourses of those who are in error, for he knows that gold is found mixed in gravel with dross. The money-changer suffers no harm if he puts his hand into the counterfeiter's purse ; relying on his skill he picks the true gold from among the spurious and counterfeit coins. It is only the simple villager, not the experienced money-changer, who is made to abstain from dealings with the counterfeiter. It is not the strong swimmer who is kept back from the shore, but the clumsy tiro ; not the accomplished snake-charmer who is barred from touching the snake, but the ignorant boy.

The majority of men, I maintain, are dominated by a high opinion of their own skill and accomplishments, especially the perfection of their intellects for distinguishing true from false and sure guidance from misleading suggestion. It is therefore necessary, I maintain, to shut the gate so as to keep the general public from reading the books of the misguided as far as possible. The public are not free from the infection of the second bad tendency we are about to discuss, even if they are uninfected by the one just mentioned.

To some of the statements made in our published works on the principles of the religious sciences an objection has been raised by a group of men whose understanding has not fully grasped the sciences and whose insight has not penetrated to the fundamentals of the systems. They think that these statements are taken from the works of the ancient philosophers, whereas the fact is that some of them are the product of reflections which occurred to me independently—it is not improbable that one shoe should fall on another shoe-mark—while others come from the revealed Scriptures, and in the case of the majority the sense though perhaps not the actual words is found in the works of the mystics.

Suppose, however, that the statements are found only in the philosophers' books. If they are reasonable in themselves and supported by proof, and if they do not contradict the Book and the Sunnah (the example of Muhammad), then it is not necessary to abstain from using them. If we open this door, if we adopt the attitude of abstaining from every truth that the mind of a heretic has apprehended before us, we should be obliged to abstain from much that is true. We should be obliged to leave aside a great number of the verses of the Qur'an and the Traditions of the Messenger and the accounts of the early Muslims, and all the sayings of the philosophers and the mystics. The reason for that is that the author of the book of the 'Brethren of Purity' has cited them in his work. He argues from them, and 104 by means of them he has gradually enticed men of weaker understanding to accept his falsehoods ; he goes on making those claims until the heretics wrest truth from our hands by thus depositing it in their writings.

The lowest degree of education is to distinguish oneself from the ignorant ordinary man. The educated man does not loathe honey even if he finds it in the surgeon's cupping-glass ; he realizes that the cupping-glass does not essentially alter the honey. The natural aversion from it in such a case rests on popular ignorance, arising from the fact that the cupping-glass is made only for impure blood. Men imagine that the 105 blood is impure because it is in the cupping-glass, and are not aware that the impurity is due to a property

41

of the blood itself. Since this property is absent from the honey, the fact that the honey is in such a container does not produce this property in it. Impurity, therefore, should not be attributed to the honey. To do so is fanciful and false.

Yet this is the prevalent idea among the majority of men. Wherever one ascribes a statement to an author of whom they approve, they accept it, even although it is false ; wherever one ascribes it to an author of whom they disapprove, they reject it even although it is true. They always make the man the criterion of truth and not truth the criterion of the man ; and that is erroneous in the extreme.

This is the wrong tendency towards rejection of the ethics of the philosophers.

(b) There is also a wrong tendency towards accepting it. When a man looks into their books, such as the 'Brethren of Purity' and others, and sees how, mingled with their teaching, are maxims of the prophets and utterances of the mystics, he often approves of these, and accepts them and forms a high opinion of them. Next, however, he readily accepts the falsehood they mix with that, because of the good opinion resulting from what he noticed and approved. That is a way of gradually slipping into falsehood.

Because of this tendency it is necessary to abstain from reading their books on account of the deception and danger in them. Just as the poor swimmer must be kept from the slippery banks, so must mankind be kept from reading these books ; just as the boy must be kept from touching the snake, so must the ears be kept from receiving such utterances. Indeed, just as tne snake-charmer must refrain from touching the snake in front of his small boy, because he knows that the boy imagines he is like his father and will imitate him, and

106

42

must even caution the boy by himself showing caution in front of him, so the first-rate scholar too must act in similar fashion. And just as the good snake-charmer on receiving a snake distinguishes between the antidote and the poison, and extracts the antidote while destroying the poison, and would not withhold the antidote from any in need ; and just as the acute and experienced money-changer, after putting his hand into the bag of the counterfeiter and extracting from it the pure gold and throwing away the spurious and counterfeit coins, would not withhold the good and acceptable money from one in need; even so does the scholar act.

Again, when a man has been bitten by a snake and needs the antidote, his being turns from it in loathing because he learns it is extracted from the snake, the source of the poison, and he requires to be shown the value of the antidote despite its source. Likewise, a poor man in need of money, who shrinks from receiving the gold taken out the bag of the counterfeiter, ought to have it brought to his notice that his shrinking is pure ignorance and is the cause of his missing the benefit he seeks ; he ought to be informed that the proximity between the counterfeit and the good coin does not make the good coin counterfeit nor the counterfeit good. In the same way the proximity between truth and falsehood does not make truth falsehood nor falsehood truth.

This much we wanted to say about the baneful and mischievous influence of philosophy.

3. *The Danger of 'Authoritative Instruction'*.

By the time I had done with the science of philosophy —acquiring an understanding of it and marking what was spurious in it—I had realized that this too did not

109 satisfy my aim in full and that the intellect neither comprehends all it attempts to know nor solves all its problems. The heresy of the Ta'līmīyah had already appeared, and everyone was speaking about their talk of gaining knowledge of the meaning of things from an infallible Imam who has charge of the truth. It had already occurred to me to study their views and become acquainted with what is in their books, when it happened that I received a definite command from His Majesty the Caliph to write a book showing what their religious system really is. The fact that I could not excuse myself from doing this was an external motive reinforcing the original impulse from within. I began to search for their books and collect their doctrines. There had already come to my ears some of their novel utterances, the product of the thoughts of contemporary members of the sect, which differed from the familiar formulations of their predecessors.

I made a collection, then, of these utterances, arranged them in logical order and formulated them correctly. I also gave a complete answer to them. In consequence some of the orthodox (*Ahl al-Ḥaqq*) criticized me for my painstaking restatement of their arguments. 'You are doing their work for them', they said, 'for they would have been unable to uphold their system in view of these dubious and ambiguous utterances had you not restated them and put them in order'.

In a way this criticism is justified. Aḥmad b. Ḥanbal
110 once criticized al-Ḥārith al-Muḥāsibī (may God have mercy on them !) for his book, *The Refutation of the Mu'tazilah*. 'It is a duty to refute heresy', al-Ḥārith replied. 'Certainly', said Aḥmad, 'but you first give an account of their false doctrines and afterwards a refutation of them. How can you be sure what men will do ? A man might read the false doctrines and grasp them

with his understanding without turning afterwards to the refutation; or he might peruse the refutation without understanding its full import'.

Aḥmad's observation is justified, but it applies to false doctrine which is not widely and generally known. Where such doctrine is widely known, it ought to be refuted, and refutation presupposes a statement of the doctrine. Certainly, no one should undertake to elaborate on their behalf a false doctrine which they have not elaborated. I personally did not do that. I had already heard that false doctrine from one of a group of those who frequented my company after having been in contact with them and having adopted their faith. He related how they used to laugh at the works composed to refute their views, since the authors had not comprehended their proof; he mentioned that proof and gave a summary of it. As I could not be satisfied with the prospect that I might be suspected of neglecting the essential basis of their proof, or of having heard it and failed to understand it, I repeated it in my book. My aim was to repeat their false doctrine as far as possible, and then to bring out its weak points.

The result was that there was no result on the part of the opponents and no force in their argument, and, had it not been for the mistaken help given by honest but ignorant men, that heresy would have been too weak to reach its present degree of success. Violent fanaticism, however, provoked the supporters of the truth to prolong the debate with them about the presuppositions of their argument and to deny all they assert. In particular they denied both their claim that 'there is need of "authoritative instruction" (ta'līm) and an instructor (mu'allim)', and their claim that 'not every instructor is adequate, there must be an infallible instructor'.

45

Now, their demonstration of the need for instruction
and an instructor was clearly sound, while the retort of
the critics was weak. A number of people were thus
deceived into thinking that this was due to the strength
of the system of the Ta'līmīyah and to the weakness of
that of their opponents. They did not realize that this
state of a affairs was due to the weakness of the defender
of the truth and his ignorance of the proper method of
dealing with the question.

The correct procedure is in fact to acknowledge the
need for an instructor and the necessity of his being
112 infallible. But our infallible instructor is Muhammad
(peace be upon him). They may say, 'He is dead'; but
we reply, 'Your instructor is hidden (ghā'ib)'. They may
say, 'Our instructor instructed the preachers and
spread them widely through the land, and, if they
differ or are puzzled by a difficulty, he expects them to
return to him'; but we reply, 'Our instructor instructed
the preachers and spread them widely through the
land and perfected the instruction, according to the
word of God most high, 'Today I have perfected your
religion for you' (Q. 5, 5); when the instruction has
been made perfect, the death of the instructor does no
harm, any more than does his being hidden'.

There remains their argument: 'How do you judge
about what you have not heard (sc. a point of law on
which there has been no explicit ruling)? Is it by the
letter of the law (nass)? But ex hypothesi you have not
heard it. Is it by your independent interpretation
(ijtihād) and opinion (ra'y)? That is precisely the place
where differences occur.'

To this we reply: 'We do what Mu'ādh did when the
Apostle of God (peace be upon him) sent him to the
113 Yemen; we judge by the actual text where there is a
text, and by our independent reasoning where there is

46

no text.[1] That is exactly what their preachers do when they are away from the Imam at the remotest corners of the land. They cannot in all cases judge by the text, for the texts which are finite in number cannot deal with all the infinite variety of events ; nor is it possible for them to return to the city of the Imam over every difficult case—while the preacher is travelling there and back the person concerned may have died, and the journey will have been fruitless.

For instance, if a man is in doubt about the *qiblah*,[2] the only course open to him is to pray according to his independent judgement. If he were to go to the city of the Imam to obtain a knowledge of the *qiblah*, the time of prayer would be past. As a matter of fact prayer fulfils the law even when directed to what is wrongly supposed to be the *qiblah*. There is the saying that the man who is mistaken in independent judgement receives a reward, but the man who is correct a twofold reward ; and that is the case in all questions left to independent judgement.

Another example of the same is the giving of alms to the poor. A man by his independent judgement will often suppose the recipient poor although he is really rich and hides his wealth. The giver of alms is not punished for this, though he was mistaken ; he is liable to punishment only for the motive leading him to make the supposition (*sc.* his resolution to give alms)'.

It may be said to us : 'The supposition of a man's opponent is as good as his own'. We reply : 'A man is

---

[1] Al-Ghazāli refers to a well-known story about Muʻādh b. Jabal. Muhammad, on appointing him as judge in the Yemen, questioned him about the principles on which he would base his rulings ; he replied that he would base them firstly on the text of the Qur'an, then, if no text was applicable, on the Sunnah of the Prophet, then, if neither was available, on the independent exercise of his judgement.

[2] The direction in which Mecca lies, in which a Muslim must face in saying his prayers.

commanded to follow his own opinion; just as in the case of the *qiblah*, the man exercising independent judgement follows his own opinion even if others differ from him'.

Again it may be said (to us): 'The man who accepts authority in all legal matters (*muqallid*) follows either Abū Ḥanīfah or al-Shāfiʿī (may God have mercy on them) or someone else (*sc.* and so you admit the principle of 'authoritative instruction')'. I reply: 'What does such a man do in the question of the *qiblah* where there is dubiety and the independently-judging authorities differ'? My opponent will say: 'The man must use his own judgement to decide which is the soundest authority and the most learned in the proofs of the *qiblah*, and then he follows his own decision'. Exactly the same happens in deciding between religious systems (*sc.* and so the principle of 'authoritative instruction' is admitted to be inadequate).

Prophets and religious leaders of necessity made mankind have recourse to independent judgement, even although they knew that they might fall into error. Indeed the Messenger of God (peace be upon him) said, 'I judge by externals, but God administers the inmost hearts'; that is to say, 'I judge by the more probable opinion, based on the account of the witnesses, but the witnesses may be mistaken'. The prophets had no way to obviate error in the case of such matters of independent judgement. So how can we hope to attain that?

There are two questions which the Taʿlīmīyah raise at this point. (1) One is this argument of theirs: 'Even if this is the case in matters of independent judgement, it is not the case with regard to fundamental beliefs. Any mistake there is not to be excused. How then is a man to proceed'? I reply: 'The fundamental beliefs are contained in the Book and the Sunnah; in questions of detail and other disputed matters apart from these fundamentals the truth is known by weighing them in 'the just balance', that is, the standards set forth by God most high in His Book; and they are five in number as I show in *The Just Balance*.

It may be said to me : 'Your adversaries do not agree with you about the standard'. I reply : 'It is not to be imagined that anyone who understands that standard should be in disagreement about it. The Ta'līmīyah will not disagree about it, because I have inferred it from the Qur'an and learnt it there; the logicians will not disagree about it because it is in accordance, not in disagreement, with the conditions they lay down in logic; the theologians will not disagree about it because it is in accordance with their views about the proof of speculative propositions, and provides a criterion of the truth of theological assertions'.

My adversary may say : 'If you have in your hand a standard such as this, why do you not remove the disagreement among mankind'? I reply : 'If they were to give heed to me, I would remove the disagreement among them. I described the method of removing disagreement in *The Just Balance*. Study it and you will find that it is sound and does completely remove disagreement if men pay attention to it; but they will not all pay attention to it. Still a group of men have paid attention to me and I removed the disagreement between them. Now your Imam wants to remove the disagreement between them although they do not pay attention to him. Why then has he not removed it ere this? Why did not 'Alī (may God be pleased with him), the first of the Imams, remove it? Does the Imam claim that he is able to bring them all forcibly to pay attention? Then why has he not so far done so? To what day has he postponed it? Is not the only result of his claim

116

4   49

that there are more disputes among mankind and more who dispute? The disagreement certainly gave grounds for fearing that evils would increase until blood was shed, towns reduced to ruins, children orphaned, communications cut and goods plundered. What has actually happened is that throughout the world such blessings have attended your removal of disagreement that there is now disagreement the like of which has never before been seen'.

The adversary may say: 'You claim that you remove the disagreement among mankind. But the man who is in doubt about the merits of the rival systems is not obliged to listen to you rather than to your opponents. The majority of your opponents disagree with you; and there is no vital difference between them and you'. This is their second question.

117   I reply : 'First of all, this argument turns back against yourself. If you summon the man in doubt to accept your own views, he will say, 'On what grounds are you to be preferred to your opponents, seeing that the majority of scholars disagree with you'? Would that I knew what answer you will give ! Will you reply by saying, 'My Imam is established by the very words of Scriptures'? Who will believe this claim to have a scriptural basis, when he has not heard the words from the Messenger? All that he has heard is your claim, and the unanimous judgment of scholars that it is an invention and to be disbelieved.

Let us suppose, however, that this scriptural claim is granted. Let the man may still have doubts on the subject of prophethood; he may say, 'Grant that your Imam adduces as proof the miracle of Jesus; that is, he says, 'The proof of my truthfulness is that I will bring your father to life'; he actually restores him to life and says to me that he is performing what he promised.

50

How do I know that he is truthful? This miracle has not brought all mankind to know the truthfulness of Jesus. On the contrary, serious objections can be raised against it, which are only to be repelled by detailed rational considerations. Rational considerations, however, are not to be trusted, according to your view. Yet no one knows the argument from miracle to truthfulness unless he knows magic and the distinction between that and miracle, and unless he knows that God does not lead His servants astray. The topic of God's leading men astray is one where it is notoriously difficult to make a reply. How then can you rebut all these objections when there is no reason for following your Imam rather than his opponent? The matter comes back to the intellectual proofs which you deny; and your adversary adduces proofs similar to yours but clearer'.

118

Thus this topic turns back against themselves so decisively that, even if the older and younger members of the sect agreed to give an answer, they would be unable to do so. The corrupt doctrine has grown apace only because a group of inferior intellects argued against them and employed the method of 'reply' (*jawāb*) instead of that of 'reversal' (*qalb*) (*sc.* tried to reply to objections to their own views instead of finding inconsistencies in the opponents' assertions). Such a procedure prolongs the debate and neither readily convinces men's minds nor effectively silences the opponents.

Some one may say: 'This is 'reversal'; but is there any 'reply' to that'? I answer : 'Certainly. The reply is that, if the man in doubt says, 'I am in doubt', and does not specify the topic about which he is in doubt, it may be said to him, 'You are like a sick man who says, 'I am sick', without specifying his disease, and yet asks for a remedy; he has to be told, 'There does not exist any remedy for disease in general but only for specific diseases like headache, diarrhoea and so forth''. Similarly the man in doubt must specify what he is in doubt about. If he specifies the topic, I show him the truth about it by weighing it by the five standards which everyone who understands them acknowledges to be the true balance on which men rely whenever they weigh anything. The balance and the soundness of the weighing are understood in just the same way as the student of arithmetic understands both arithmetic and the fact that the teacher of arithmetic knows the subject and speaks truly about it'. I have explained that in *The Just Balance* in the compass of twenty pages, and it may be studied there.

My object at the moment is not to show the falsity of their views, for I have already done so (1) in *Al-Mustazhirī*, (2) in *The Demonstration of Truth*, a reply to criticisms made against me in Baghdad, (3) in *The Fundamental Difference* (*between Islam and Unbelief*), in twelve chapters, a reply to criticisms made against me in Hamadān, (4) in the book of the *Durj* drawn up in tabular form, which deals with the feeble criticisms of me made in Ṭūs, and (5) in *The Just Balance*, which is an independent work intended to show what is the standard by which knowledge is weighed and how the man who has comprehended this has no need of an infallible Imam.

My present aim is rather to show that the Bāṭinīyah have nothing to cure them or save them from the darkness of mere opinions. Their inability to demonstrate that a specific person is Imam is not their only weakness. We went a long way in agreeing with them; we accepted their assertion that 'instruction' is needed and an infallible 'instructor'; we conceded that he is the one they specified. Yet when we asked them what knowledge they had gained from this infallible person, and raised objections against them, they did not understand these, far less answer them, and in their perplexity had recourse to the 'hidden Imam' and said one must journey to see him. The astonishing thing is that they squander their lives in searching for the 'instructor' and in boasting that they have found him, yet without learning anything at all from him. They are like a man smeared with filth, who so wearies himself with the search for water that when he comes upon it he does not use it but remains smeared with dirt.

There are indeed certain of them who lay claim to have some special knowledge. But this knowledge, as they describe it, amounts to some trifling details of the philosophy of Pyhthagoras. The latter was one of the earliest of the ancients and his philosophical system is the weakest of all; Aristotle not only criticized him but showed the weakness and corruption of his thought. Yet he is the person followed in the *Book of the Brethren of Purity*, which is really but the dregs of philosophy.

It is truly amazing that men should toil all their life long searching for knowledge and in the end be content with such feeble and emaciated knowledge, while imagining that they have attained the utmost aims of the sciences ! These claimants to knowledge also we have examined, probing into both external and internal features of their views. All they amounted to was a deception of the ordinary man and the weak intellect by proving the need for an 'instructor'. Their further arguments to show that there is no need for instruction by theological reasoning are strong and unanswerable until one tries to help them to prove the need for an 'instructor' by saying, 'Give us some examples of his knowledge and of his "instruction".' Then the exponent ᵼs at a loss. 'Now that you have submitted this difficulty to me', he says, 'I shall search for a solution; my present object, however, is limited to what I have already said'. He knows that, if he were to attempt to proceed further, his shameful condition would be revealed and he would be unable to resolve the least of the problems —that he would be unable even to understand them, far less to answer them.

This is the real condition in which they are. As it is said, 'Try them and you will hate them'!—after we had tried them we left them also severely alone.

122   4. *The Ways of Mysticism.*

When I had finished with these sciences, I next turned with set purpose to the method of mysticism (or Sufism). I knew that the complete mystic 'way' includes both intellectual belief and practical activity; the latter consists in getting rid of the obstacles in the self and in stripping off its base characteristics and vicious morals, so that the heart may attain to freedom from what is not God and to constant recollection of Him.

The intellectual belief was easier to me than the practical activity. I began to acquaint myself with their belief by reading their book, such as *The Food of*
123 *the Hearts* by Abū Ṭālib al-Makkī (God have mercy upon him), the works of al-Ḥārith al-Muḥāsibī, the
124 various anecdotes about al-Junayd, ash-Shiblī and Abū Yazīd al-Bisṭāmī (may God sanctify their spirits), and other discourses of their leading men. I thus comprehended their fundamental teachings on the intellectual side, and progressed, as far as is possible by study and oral instruction, in the knowledge of mysticism. It became clear to me, however, that what is most distinctive of mysticism is something which cannot be

54

apprehended by study, but only by immediate experience (*dhawq*—literally 'tasting'), by ecstasy and by a moral change. What a difference there is between *knowing* the definition of health and satiety, together with their causes and presuppositions, and *being*, healthy and satisfied! What a difference between being acquainted with the definition of drunkenness—namely, that it designates a state arising from the domination of the seat of the intellect by vapours arising from the stomach —and being drunk! Indeed, the drunken man while in that condition does not know the definition of drunkenness nor the scientific account of it; he has not the very least scientific knowledge of it. The sober man, on the other hand, knows the definition of drunkenness and its basis, yet he is not drunk in the very least. Again the doctor, when he is himself ill, knows the definition and causes of health and the remedies which restore it, and yet is lacking in health. Similarly there is a difference between knowing the true nature and causes and conditions of the ascetic life and actually leading such a life and forsaking the world.

I apprehended clearly that the mystics were men who had real experiences, not men of words, and that I had already progressed as far as was possible by way of intellectual apprehension. What remained for me was not to be attained by oral instruction and study but only by immediate experience and by walking in the mystic way.

Now from the sciences I had laboured at and the paths I had traversed in my investigation of the revelational and rational sciences (that is, presumably, theology and philosophy), there had come to me a sure faith in God most high, in prophethood (or revelation), and in the Last Day. These three credal principles were firmly rooted in my being, not through any carefully argued proof, but by reason of various causes, coincidences and experiences which are not capable of being stated in detail.

It had already become clear to me that I had no hope of the bliss of the world to come save through a God-fearing life and the withdrawal of myself from vain desire. It was clear to me too that the key to all this was to serve the attachment of the heart to worldly things by leaving the mansion of deception and returning to that of eternity, and to advance towards God most high with all earnestness. It was also clear that this was only to be achieved by turning away from wealth and position and fleeing from all time-consuming entanglements.

Next I considered the circumstances of my life, and realized that I was caught in a veritable thicket of attachments. I also considered my activities, of which the best was my teaching and lecturing, and realized that in them I was dealing with sciences that were unimportant and contributed nothing to the attainment of eternal life.

After that I examined my motive in my work of teaching, and realized that it was not a pure desire for the things of God, but that the impulse moving me was the desire for an influential position and public recognition. I saw for certain that I was on the brink of a crumbling bank of sand in imminent danger of hell-fire unless I set about to mend my ways.

I reflected on this continuously for a time, while the choice still remained open to me. One day I would form the resolution to quit Baghdad and get rid of these adverse circumstances; the next day I would abandon my resolution. I put one foot forward and drew the other back. If in the morning I had a genuine longing to seek eternal life, by the evening the attack of a whole host of desires had reduced it to impotence. Worldly desires were striving to keep me by their chains just where I was, while the voice of faith was calling, 'To the road! to the road! What is left of life is but little and the journey before you is long. All that keeps you busy, both intellectually and practically, is but hypo- crisy and delusion. If you do not prepare *now* for eternal life, when will you prepare? If you do not now sever these attachments, when will you sever them?' On hearing that, the impulse would be stirred and the resolution made to take to flight.

Soon, however, Satan would return. 'This is a passing mood', he would say; 'do not yield to it, for it will quickly disappear; if you comply with it and leave this influential position, these comfortable and dignified circumstances where you are free from troubles and disturbances, this state of safety and security where you are untouched by the contentions of your adversaries, then you will probably come to yourself again and will not find it easy to return to all this'.

For nearly six months beginning with Rajab 488 A.H. (=July 1095 A.D.), I was continuously tossed about between the attractions of worldly desires and the impulses towards eternal life. In that month the matter ceased to be one of choice and become one of compul- sion. God caused my tongue to dry up so that I was prevented from lecturing. One particular day I would make an effort to lecture in order to gratify the hearts of my following, but my tongue would not utter a single word nor could I accomplish anything at all.

This impediment in my speech produced grief in my heart, and at the same time my power to digest and assimilate food and drink was impaired; I could hardly swallow or digest a single mouthful of food. My powers became so weakened that the doctors gave up all hope of successful treatment. 'This trouble arises from the heart', they said, 'and from there it has spread through the constitution; the only method of treatment is that the anxiety which has come over the heart should be allayad.'

Thereupon, perceiving my impotence and having altogether lost my power of choice, I sought refuge with God most high as one who is driven to Him, because he is without further resources of his own. He answered me, He who 'answers him who is driven (to Him by affliction) when he calls upon Him' (Qur'an 27, 63). He made it easy for my heart to turn away from position and wealth, from children and friends. I openly professed that I had resolved to set out for Mecca, while privately I made arrangements to travel to Syria. I took this precaution in case the Caliph and all my friends should oppose my resolve to make my residence in Syria. This stratagem for my departure from Baghdad I gracefully executed, and had it in my mind never to return there. There was much talk about me among all the religious leaders of 'Iraq, since none of them would allow that withdrawal from such a state of life as I was in could have a religious cause, for they looked upon that as the culmination of a religious career; that was the sum of their knowledge.

130　　Much confusion now came into people's minds as they tried to account for my conduct. Those at a distance from 'Iraq supposed that it was due to some apprehension I had of action by the government. On the other hand those who were close to the governing circles and had witnessed how eagerly and assiduously they sought me and how I withdrew from them and showed no great regard for what they said, would say, 'This is a supernatural affair; it must be an evil influence which has befallen the people of Islam and especially the circle of the learned'.

I left Baghdad, then, I distributed what wealth I had, retaining only as much as would suffice myself and provide sustenance for my children. This I could easily manage, as the wealth of 'Iraq was available for good works, since it constitutes a trust fund for the benefit of the Muslims. Nowhere in the world have I seen better financial arrangements to assist a scholar to provide for his children.

In due course I entered Damascus, and there I remained for nearly two years with no other occupation than the cultivation of retirement and solitude, together with religious and ascetic exercises, as I busied myself purifying my soul, improving my character and cleansing my heart for the constant recollection of God most high, as I had learnt from my study of mysticism. I used to go into retreat for a period in the mosque of Damascus, going up the minaret of the mosque for the whole day and shutting myself in so as to be alone.

131

At length I made my way from Damascus to the Holy House (that is, Jerusalem). There I used to enter into the precinct of the Rock every day and shut myself in.

Next there arose in me a prompting to fulfil the duty of the Pilgrimage, gain the blessings of Mecca and Medina, and perform the visitation of the Messenger of God most high (peace be upon him), after first performing the visitation of al-Khalīl, the Friend of God (God bless him).[1] I therefore made the journey to the Hijaz. Before long, however, various concerns, together with the entreaties of my children, drew me back to my home (country); and so I came to it again, though at

[1] That is, Abraham, who is buried in the cave of Machpelah under the mosque at Hebron, which is called 'al-Khalīl' in Arabic; similarly the visitation of the Messenger is the formal visit to his tomb at Medina.

one time no one had seemed less likely than myself to return to it. Here, too, I sought retirement, still longing for solitude and the purification of the heart for the recollection (of God). The events of the interval, the anxieties about my family, and the necessities of my livelihood altered the aspect of my purpose and impaired the quality of my solitude, for I experienced pure ecstasy only occasionally, although I did not cease to hope for that; obstacles would hold me back, yet I always returned to it.

I continued at this stage for the space of ten years, and during these periods of solitude there were revealed to me things innumerable and unfathomable. This much I shall say about that in order that others may be helped: I learnt with certainty that it is above all the mystics who walk on the road of God; their life is the best life, their method the soundest method, their character the purest character; indeed, were the intellect of the intellectuals and the learning of the learned and the scholarship of the scholars, who are versed in the profundities of revealed truth, brought together in the attempt to improve the life and character of the mystics, they would find no way of doing so ; for to the mystics all movement and all rest, whether external or internal, brings illumination from the light of the lamp of prophetic revelation ; and behind the light of prophetic revelation there is no other light on the face of the earth from which illumination may be received.

In general, then, how is a mystic 'way' (tariqah) described ? The purity which is the first condition of it (sc. as bodily purity is the prior condition of formal Worship for Muslims) is the purification of the heart completely from what is other than God most high ; the key to it, which corresponds to the opening act of adoration in prayer,[1] is the sinking of the heart completely in the recollection of God ; and the end of it is complete absorption (*fanā'*) in God. At least this is its end relatively to those first steps which almost come within the sphere of choice and personal responsibility ; but in reality in the actual mystic 'way' it is the first 133 step, what comes before it being, as it were, the antechamber for those who are journeying towards it.

With this first stage of the 'way' there begin the revelations and visions. The mystics in their waking state now behold angels and the spirits of the prophets ; they hear these speaking to them and are instructed by them. Later, a higher state is reached ; instead of beholding forms and figures, they come to stages in the 'way' which it is hard to describe in language ; if a man attempts to express these, his words inevitably contain what is clearly erroneous.

In general what they manage to achieve is nearness to God ; some, however, would conceive of this as 'inherence' (*ḥulūl*), some as 'union' (*ittiḥād*), and some as 'connection' (*wuṣūl*) 'All that is erroneous. In my book, *The Noblest Aim*, I have explained the nature of 134 the error here. Yet he who has attained the mystic 'state' need do no more than say :

Of the things I do not remember, what was, was ;

Think it good ; do not ask an account of it.

    (Ibn al-Muʿtazz).

In general the man to whom He has granted no immediate experience at all, apprehends no more of what prophetic revelation really is than the name. The miraculous graces given to the saints are in truth the beginnings of the prophets ; and that was the first

[1]Literally, the 'prohibition,' *taḥrîm*; the opening words of the Muslim Worship, 'God is great', are known as *takbîrat at-taḥrîm*, the prohibitory adoration, 'because it forbids to the worshipper what was previously allowable', Cp. Calverly, *Worship in Islam*, p. 8, etc.

'state' of the Messenger of God (peace be upon him) when he went out to Mount Ḥirā', and was given up entirely to his Lord, and worshipped, so that the bedouin said, 'Muhammad loves his Lord passionately'.

Now this is a mystical 'state' which is realized in immediate experience by those who walk in the way leading to it. Those to whom it is not granted to have immediate experience can become assured of it by trial (*sc.* contact with mystics or observation of them) and by hearsay, if they have sufficiently numerous opportunities of associating with mystics to understand that (*sc.* ecstasy) with certainty by means of what accompanies the 'states'. Whoever sits in their company derives from them this faith ; and none who sits in their company is pained.

Those to whom it is not even granted to have contacts with mystics may know with certainty the possibility of ecstasy by the evidence of demonstration, as I have remarked in the section entitled *The Wonders of the Heart* of my *Revival of the Religious Sciences*.

Certainly reached by demonstration is *knowledge* ('*ilm*) ; actual acquaintance with that 'state' is *immediate experience* (*dhawq*) ; the acceptance of it as probable from hearsay and trial (or observation) is *faith* (*imān*). These are three degrees. 'God will raise those of you who have faith and those who have been given knowledge in degrees (*sc.* of honour)' (Q. 58, 12).

Behind the mystics, however, there is a crowd of ignorant people. They deny this fundamentally, they are astonished at this line of thought, they listen and mock. 'Amazing', they say. 'What nonsense they talk' ! About such people God most high has said : 'Some of them listen to you, until, upon going out from you, they say to those to whom knowledge has been given, 'What did he say just now'? These are the people on whose

hearts God sets a seal and they follow their passions'.
(Q. 47, 18) He makes them deaf, and blinds their sight.

Among the things that necessarily became clear to
me from my practice of the mystic 'way' was the true
nature and special characteristics of prophetic revelation). The basis of that must undoubtedly be indicated in
view of the urgent need for it.

IV.   THE TRUE NATURE OF PROPHECY
AND THE COMPELLING NEED OF ALL CREATION FOR IT

You must know that the substance of man in his
original condition was created in bareness and sim-
plicity without any information about the worlds of God
most high. These worlds are many, not to be reckoned
save by God most high Himself. As He said, 'None
knows the hosts of thy Lord save He' (Q. 74, 34). Man's
information about the world is by means of perception ;
and every perception of perceptibles is created so that
thereby man may have some acquaintance with a
world (or sphere) from among existents. By 'worlds
(or spheres)' we simply mean 'classes of existents'.

The first thing created in man was the sense of *touch*,
and by it he perceives certain classes of existents, such as
heat and cold, moisture and dryness, smoothness and
roughness. Touch is completely unable to apprehend
colours and noises. These might be non-existent so far
as concerns touch.

Next there is created in him the sense of *sight*, and by
it he apprehends colours and shapes. This is the most
extensive of the worlds of sensibles. Next *hearing* is
implanted in him, so that he hears sounds of various
kinds. After that *taste* is created in him ; and so on until   138
he has completed the world of sensibles.

Next, when he is about seven years of old, there is

created in him *discernment* (or the power of distinguishing —*tamyiz*). This is a fresh stage in his development. He now apprehends more than the world of sensibles; and none of these additional factors (*sc.* relations, etc.) exists in the world of sense.

From this he ascends to another stage, and *intellect* (or reason) (*'aql*) is created in him. He apprehends things necessary, possible, impossible, things which do not occur in the previous stages.

Beyond intellect there is yet another stage. In this another eye is opened, by which he beholds the unseen, what is to be in the future, and other things which are beyond the ken of intellect in the same way as the objects of intellect are beyond the ken of the faculty of discernment and the objects of discernment are beyond the ken of sense. Morever, just as the man at the stage of discernment would reject and disregard the objects of intellect were these to be presented to him, so some intellectuals reject and disregard the objects of prophetic revelation. That is sheer ignorance. They have no ground for their view except that this is a stage which they have not reached and which for them does not exist; yet they suppose that it is non-existent in itself. When a man blind from birth, who has not learnt about colours and shapes by listening to people's talk, is told about these things for the first time, he does not understand them nor admit their existence.

God most high, however, has favoured His creatures 139 by giving them something analogous to the special faculty of prophecy, namely dreams. In the dream-state a man apprehends what is to be in the future, which is something of the unseen; he does so either explicitly or else clothed in a symbolic form whose interpretation is disclosed.

Suppose a man has not experienced this himself, and

64

suppose that he is told how some people fall into a dead faint, in which hearing, sight and the other senses no longer function, and in this condition perceive the unseen. He would deny that this is so and demonstrate its impossibility. 'The sensible powers', he would say, 'are the causes of perception (or apprehension) ; if a man does not perceive things (*sc.* the unseen) when these powers are actively present, much less will he do so when the senses are not functioning'. This is a form of analogy which is shown to be false by what actually occurs and is observed. Just as intellect is one of the stages of human development in which there is an 'eye' which sees the various types of intelligible objects, which are beyond the ken of the senses, so prophecy also is the description of a stage in which there is an eye endowed with light such that in that light the unseen and other supra-intellectual objects become visible.

Doubt about prophetic revelation is either (a) doubt of its possibility in general, or (b) doubt of its actual occurrence, or (c) doubt of the attainment of it by a specific individual.

The proof of the possibility of there being prophecy and the proof that there has been prophecy is that there is knowledge in the world the attainment of which by reason is inconceivable ; for example, in medical science and astronomy. Whoever researches in such matters knows of necessity that this knowledge is attained only by Divine inspiration and by assistance 140 from God most high. It cannot be reached by observation. For instance there are some astronomical laws based on phenomena which occur only once in a thousand years ; how can these be arrived at by personal observation? It is the same with the properties of drugs.

This argument shows that it is possible for there to be a way of apprehending these matters which are not apprehended by the intellect. This is the meaning of prophetic revelation. That is not to say that prophecy is merely an expression for such knowledge. Rather, the apprehending of this class of extra-intellectual objects is *one* of the properties of prophecy; but it has many other properties as well. The said property is but a a drop in the ocean of prophecy. It has been singled out for mention because you have something analogous to it in what you apprehend in dreaming, and because you have medical and astronomical knowledge belonging to the same class, namely, the miracles of the prophets,[1] for the intellectuals cannot arrive at these at all by any intellectual efforts.

The other properties of prophetic revelation are apprehended only by immediate experience (*dhawq*) from the practice of the mystic way, but this property of prophecy you can understand by an analogy granted you, namely, the dream-state. If it were not for the latter you would not believe in that. If the prophet possessed a faculty to which you had nothing analogous and which you did not understand, how could you believe in it ? Believing presupposes understanding. Now that analogous experience comes to a man in the early stages of the mystic way. Thereby he attains to a kind of immediate experience, extending as far as that to which he has attained, and by analogy to a kind of belief (or assent) in respect of that to which he has not attained. Thus this single property is a sufficient basis for one's faith in the principle of prophecy.

141

If you come to doubt whether a specific person is a prophet or not, certainty can only be reached by acquaintance with his conduct, either by personal

[1] This is a little obscure ; al-Ghazālī appears to regard certain miraculous signs as belonging to the spheres of medicine and astronomy ; perhaps he was thinking of this when he spoke of events occurring in a thousand years.

observation, or by hearsay as a matter of common knowledge. For example, if you are familiar with medicine and law, you can recognise lawyers and doctors by observing what they are, or, where observation is impossible, by hearing what they have to say. Thus you are not unable to recognise that al-Shāfi'ī (God have mercy upon him) is a lawyer and Galen a doctor; and your recognition is based on the facts and not on the judgement of someone else. Indeed, just because you have some knowledge of law and medicine, and examine their books and writings, you arrive at a necessary knowledge of what these men are.

Similarly, if you understand what it is to be a prophet, and have devoted much time to the study of the Qur'an and the Traditions, you will arrive at a necessary knowledge of the fact that Muhammad (God bless and preserve him) is in the highest grades of the prophetic calling. Convince yourself of that by trying out what he said about the influence of devotional practices on the purification of the heart—how truly he asserted that 'whoever lives out what he knows will receive from God what he does not know'; how truly he asserted that 'if anyone aids an evildoer, God will give that man power over him'; how truly he asserted that 'if a man rises up in the morning with but a single care (*sc.* to please God), God most high will preserve him from all cares in this world and the next'. When you have made trial of these in a thousand or several thousand instances, you will arrive at a necessary knowledge beyond all doubt.

By this method, then, seek certainty about the prophetic office, and not from the transformation of a rod into a serpent or the cleaving of the moon. For if you consider such an event by itself, without taking account of the numerous circumstances accompanying it—circumstances readily eluding the grasp of the intellect—then you might perhaps suppose that it was magic and deception and that it came from God to lead men astray; for 'He leads astray whom He will, and guides whom He will'. Thus the topic of miracles will be thrown back upon you; for if your faith is based on a reasoned argument involving the probative force of the miracle, then your faith is destroyed by an ordered argument showing the difficulty and ambiguity of the miracle.

Admit, then, that wonders of this sort are one of the proofs and accompanying circumstances out of the totality of your thought on the matter; and that you attain necessary knowledge and yet are unable to say specifically on what it is based. The case is similar to that of a man who receives from a multitude of people a piece of information which is a matter of common belief . . . He is unable to say that the certainty is derived from the remark of a single specific person; rather, its source is unknown to him; it is neither from outside the whole, nor is it from specific individuals. This is strong, intellectual faith. Immediate experience, on the other hand, is like actually witnessing a thing and taking it in one's hand. It is only found in the way of mysticism.

This is a sufficient discussion of the nature of prophetic revelation for my present purpose. I proceed to speak of the need for it.

144 V. THE REASON FOR TEACHING AGAIN AFTER MY WITHDRAWAL FROM IT

I had persevered thus for nearly ten years in retirement and solitude. I had come of necessity—from reasons which I do not enumerate, partly immediate experience, partly demonstrative knowledge, partly acceptance in faith—to a realization of various truths.

I saw that man was constituted of body and heart; by 'heart' I mean the real nature of his spirit which is the seat of his knowledge of God, and not the flesh and blood which he shares with the corpse and the brute beast. I saw that just as there is health and disease in the body, respectively causing it to prosper and to perish, so also there is in the heart, on the one hand, health and soundness—and 'only he who comes to God with a sound heart' (Q. 26, 89) is saved—and, on the other hand, disease, in which is eternal and other worldly destruction—as God most high says, 'in their hearts is disease' (Q. 2, 9). I saw that to be ignorant of God is destructive poison, and to disobey Him by following desire is the thing which produces the disease, while to know God most high is the life-giving antidote and to 145 obey Him by opposing desire is the healing medicine. I saw, too, that the only way to treat the heart, to end its disease and procure its health, is by medicines, just as that is the only way of treating the body.

Moreover, the medicines of the body are effective in producing health through some property in them which the intellectuals do not apprehend with their intellectual apparatus, but in respect of which one must accept the statement of the doctors; and these in turn are dependent on the prophets who by the property of prophethood have grasped the properties of things. Similarly I came of necessity to realize that in the case of the medicines of formal worship, which have been fixed and determined by the prophets, the manner of their effectiveness is not apprehended by the intellectual explanations of the intellectuals; one must rather accept the statements (taqlīd) of the prophets who apprehended those properties by the light of prophecy, not by intellectual explanation.

Again, medicines are composed of ingredients differing in kind and quantity—one, for instance, is twice another in weight and amount; and this quantitative difference involve secret lore of the same type as knowledge of the properties. Similariy, formal worship, which is the medicine for the disease of the heart is compounded of acts differing in kind and amount; the prostration (*sujūd*) is the double of the bowing (*rukū'*) in amount, and the morning worship half of the afternoon worship; and such arrangements are not without a mystery of the same type as the properties which are grasped by the light of prophecy. Indeed a man is very foolish and very ignorant if he tries to show by intellectual means that these arrangements are wise, or if he fancies that they are specified accidentally and not from a Divine mystery in them which fixes them by way of the property.

Yet again, medicines have bases, which are the principal active ingredients, and 'additions' (auxiliaries or correctives), which are complementary, each of them having its specific influence on the action of the bases. Similarly, the supererogatory practices and the 'customs' are complements which perfect the efficacy of the basic elements of formal worship.

In general, the prophets are the physicians of the diseases of hearts. The only advantage of the intellect is that it informed us of that, bearing witness to prophetic revelation by believing (*sc.* the trustworthiness of the prophets) and to itself by being unable to apprehend what is apprehended by the eye of prophecy; then it took us by the hand and entrusted us to prophetic revelation, as the blind are entrusted to their guides and anxious patients to sympathetic doctors. Thus far may the intellect proceed. In what lies beyond it has no part, save in the understanding of what the physician communicates to it.

145

These, then, are matters which we learnt by a
necessity like that of direct vision in the period of
solitude and retirement.

We next observed the laxity of men's belief in the
principle of prophecy and in its actuality and in conduct
according to the norms elucidated by prophecy; we
ascertained that this was widespread among the people.
When I considered the reasons for people's laxity and
weakness of faith, I found there were four:

(a) a reason connected with those who engage in
     philosophy;

(b) a reason connected with those who engage in
     the mystic way;

(c) a reason connected with those who profess the
     doctrine of *ta'līm*;

(d) a reason based on the practice of those who are
     popularly described as having knowledge.

For a time I went after individual men, questioning
those who fell short in observing the Law. I would
question one about his doubts and investigate his inmost
beliefs. 'Why is it', I said, 'that you fall short in that?
If you believe in the future life and, instead of preparing
for it, sell it in order to buy this world, then that is folly!
You do not normally sell two things for one; how can
you give up an endless life for a limited number of days?
If, on the other hand, you do not believe in it, then you
are an infidel! Dispose yourself to faith. Observe what
is the cause of your hidden unbelief, for that is the
doctrinal system you inwardly adopt and the cause of
your outward daring, even though you do not give
expression to it out of respect towards the faith and
reverence for the mention of the law!'

(1) One would say: 'If it were obligatory to observe
this matter, then those learned in religious questions
would be foremost in doing so; but, among persons of

distinction, A does not perform the Worship, B drinks wine, C devours the property of trusts and orphans, D accepts the munificence of the sovereign and does not refrain from forbidden things, E accepts bribes for giving judgement or bearing witness; and so on'.

A second man claims to have knowledge of mysticism and considers that he has made such progress that he is above the need for formal worship.

A third man is taken up with another of the doubts of the 'Latitudinarians' (*Ahl al-Ibāḥah*; cp. *Encyclopaedia of Islam*, s.v. 'Ibaḥīya'). These are those who stray from the path of mysticism.

(2) A fourth man, having met the party of *ta'līm* would say: 'Truth is difficult, the way to it blocked, and the disputes over it numerous. No one system of doctrine is preferable to any other. Rational proofs contradict one another, and no confidence can be placed in the speculations of the speculative thinkers (*ashāb al-ra'y*). He who summons to *ta'līm* makes assertions without proof. How then through doubt can I keep certainty ?

149 (3) A fifth man says: 'I do not perform these acts out of obedience to authority (*taqlīdan*). I have studied philosophy and I know that prophecy actually exists and that its achievement is wise and beneficial. I see that the acts of worship it prescribes aim at keeping order among the common people and restraining them from fighting and quarreling with one another and from giving rein to their desires. But I am not one of the ignorant common people that I should enter within the narrow confines of duty. On the contrary I am one of the wise, I follow wisdom, and thereby see clearly (for myself) so that I do not require to follow authority'.

This is the final word of the faith of those who study the system of the theistic philosophers, as you may learn from the works of Ibn Sīnā and ̦Abū Naṣr al-Fārābī.

72

These are the people who show politeness to Islam. Often you see one of them reading the Qur'an, attending the Friday assembly and public Worship and praising the sacred Law. Nevertheless he does not refrain from drinking wine and from various wicked and immoral practices ! If someone says to him, 'If the prophetic revelation is not genuine, why do you join in the prayers'? perhaps he will reply, 'To exercise my body, and because it is a custom in the place, and to keep my wealth and family'. Or perhaps he says, 'The sacred Law is genuine; the prophetic revelation is true'; then he is asked, 'And why then do you drink wine'? and he replies, 'Wine is forbidden only because it leads to enmity and hatred ; I am sufficiently wise to guard against that, and so I take wine to make my mind more lively'. Ibn Sīnā actually writes in his *Testament* that he swore to God that he would do various things, and in particular that he would praise what the sacred Law prescribed, that he would not be lax in taking part in the public worship of God, and that he would not drink for pleasure but only as a tonic or medicine. Thus the net result of his purity of faith and observance of the obligations of worship was that he made an exception of drinking wine for medical purposes !

150

Such is the faith of those philosophers who profess religious faith. Many have been deceived by them; and the deceit has been the greater because of the ineffectiveness of the criticism levelled against the philosophers, since that consisted, as we have shown above, in denying geometry and logic and others of their sciences which possess necessary truth.

I observed, then, to what an extent and for what reasons faith was weak among the various classes of men; and I observed how I myself was occupied with the resolving of this doubt, indeed I had devoted so

73

much time and energy to the study of their sciences and methods—I mean those of the mystics, the philosophers, the 'authoritarian instructionists' (ta'limiyah) and the outstanding scholars (mutawassimun)—that to show up their errors was easier for me than drinking water. As I observed all this, the impression was formed in me: 'That is a fixed and determinate character of this time; what benefit to you, then, are solitude and retirement, since the sickness has become general, the doctors have fallen ill, and mankind has reached the verge of destruction?' I said to myself, however: 'When will you busy yourself in resolving these difficulties and attacking these obscurities; seeing it is an age of slackness, an era of futility? Even if you were to labour at summoning men from their worthless ways to the truth, the people of this age would be united in showing hostility to you. How will you stand up to them? How will you live among them, seeing that such a project is only to be executed with the aid of time and through a pious sovereign who is all-powerful?'

I believed that it was permissible for me in the sight of God to continue in retirement on the ground of my inability to demonstrate the truth by argument. But God most high determined Himself to stir up the impulse of the sovereign of the time, though not by any external means; the latter gave me strict orders to hasten to Naysābūr (Nīshāpūr) to tackle the problem of this lukewarmness in religious matters. So strict was the injunction that, had I persisted in disobeying it, I should at length have been cut off! I came to realize, too, that the grounds which had made retirement permissible had lost their force. 'It is not right that your motive for clinging to retirement should be laziness and love of ease, the quest for spiritual power and preservation from worldly contamination. It was not because of the difficulty of restoring men to health that you gave yourself this permission'.

Now God most high says: 'In the name of God, the 152 Merciful, the Compassionate. Alif, Lām, Mīm. Do the people think that they will be left in the position that they say, 'We have believed', without their being tried? We tried those who were before them' (Q. 29, 1), and what follows. He (may He be exalted!) says to His messenger, who is the noblest of His creatures: 'Messengers have been counted false before thee, but they patiently endured the falsehood laid to their charge and the insults done them, until Our help came to them; no one can change the words of God, and surely there has come to thee some information about those who were sent (as messengers).' (Q. 6, 34). He (may He be exalted) says too: 'In the name of God, the Merciful, the Compassionate. Yā', Sīn. By the Qur'an that decides . . . Thou wilt only warn him who follows the Reminder' (Q. 36, 1 and 11).

On this matter I consulted a number of men skilled in the science of the heart and with experience of contemplation. They unanimously advised me to abandon my retirement and leave the zāwiyah (hospice). My resolution was further strengthened by numerous visions of good men in all of which alike I was given the assurance that this impulse was a source of good, was genuine guidance, and had been determined by God most high for the beginning of this century; for God most high has promised to revive His religion at the beginning of each century.[1] My hope became strong, and all these considerations caused the favour- 153 able view of the project to prevail.

[1]There was a well-known Tradition to the effect that at the beginning of each century God would send a man to revive religion. The events in question took place a few months before the beginning of the sixth century A.H.

God most high facilitated my move to Naysābūr to deal with this serious problem in Dhu'l-Qa'dah, the eleventh month of 499 (=July, 1106 A.D.). I had originally left Baghdad in Dhu'l-Qa'dah, 488, (= November, 1095), so that my period of retirement had extended to eleven years. It was God most high who determined this move, and it is an example of the wonderful way in which He determines events, since there was not a whisper of it in my heart while I was living in retirement. In the same way my departure from Baghdad and withdrawal from my position there had not even occurred to my mind as a possibility. But God is the upsetter of hearts[1] and positions. As the Tradition has it, 'The heart of the believer is between two of the fingers of the Merciful'.

In myself I know that, even if I went back to the work of disseminating knowledge, yet I did not go back. To go back is to return to the previous state of things. Previously, however, I had been disseminating the knowledge by which worldly success is attained; by word and deed I had called men to it; and that had been my aim and intention. But now I am calling men to the knowledge whereby worldly success is given up and its low position in the scale of real worth is recognized. 154 This is now my intention, my aim, my desire; God knows that this is so. It is my earnest longing that I may make myself and others better. I do not know whether I shall reach my goal or whether I shall be taken away while short of my object. I believe, however, both by certain faith and by intuition that there is no power and no might save with God, the high, the mighty, and that I do not move of myself but am moved by Him, I do not work of myself but am used by Him. I ask Him first of all to reform me and then to reform through me, to

[1] *Muqallib al-qulūb*—with a play on the words.

guide me and then to guide through me, to show me the truth of what is true and to grant of His bounty that I may follow it, and to show me the falsity of what is false and to grant of His bounty that I may turn away from it.

We now return to the earlier topic of the causes for the weakness of faith, and consider how to guide men aright and deliver them from the perils they face. '

For those who profess perplexity as a result of what they have heard from the party of *ta'lim*, the treatment is that prescribed in our book, *The Just Balance*, and we shall not lengthen this essay by repeating it.

As for the fanciful assertions of the Latitudinarians *Ahl al-Ibāḥah*), we have collected their doubts under seven heads, and resolved them, in our book, *The Chemistry of Happiness*.

In reply to those who through philosophy have corrupted their faith to the extent of denying prophecy in principle, we have discussed the reality of prophecy and how it exists of necessity, by showing that there exists a knowledge of the properties of medicines, stars, and so forth. We introduced this preliminary study precisely for this purpose; we based the demonstration on medical and astronomical properties precisely because these are included in the science of the Philosophers. To every one who is expert in some branch of science, be it astronomy (? astrology) or medicine, physics, magic or charm-making, we offer proof of prophecy based on his own branch of science.

The man who verbally professes belief in prophecy, but equates the prescriptions of the revealed scriptures with (philosophic) wisdom, really disbelieves in prophecy, and believes only in a certain judge (v.l. philosopher) the ascendancy of whose star is such that it determines men to follow him. This is not prophecy at all. On the contrary, faith in prophecy is to acknowledge the existence of a sphere beyond reason; into this sphere an eye penetrates whereby man apprehends special objects-of-apprehension. From these reason is excluded in the same way as the hearing is excluded from apprehending colours and sight from apprehending sounds and all the senses from apprehending the objects-of-reason.

If our opponent does not admit this, well, we have given a demonstration that a suprarational sphere is possible, indeed that it actually exists. If, however, he admits our contention, he has affirmed the existence of things called properties with which the operations of reason are not concerned at all; indeed, reason almost denies them and judges them absurd. For instance, the weight of a *dāniq* (about eight grains) of opium is a deadly poison, freezing the blood in the veins through its excess of cold. The man who claims a knowledge of physics considers that when a composite substance becomes cold it always does so through the two elements of water and earth, since these are the cold elements. It is well-known, however, that many pounds of water and earth are not productive of cold in the interior of the body to the same extent as this weight of opium. If a physicist were informed of this fact, and had not discovered it by experiment, he would say, 'This is impossible; the proof of its impossibility is that the opium contains the elements of fire and air, and these elements do not increase cold; even supposing it was entirely composed of water and earth, that would not necessitate this extreme freezing action, much less does it do so when the two hot elements are joined with them'. He supposes that this is a proof!

Most of the philosophers' proofs in natural science and theology are constructed in this fashion. They conceive of things according to the measure of their observations and reasonings. What they are unfamiliar with they suppose impossible. If it were not that veridical vision in sleep is familiar, then, when someone claimed to gain knowledge of the unseen while his senses were at rest, men with such intellects would deny it. If you said to one, 'Is it possible for there to be in the world a thing, the size of a grain, which, if placed in a town, will consume that town in its entirety and then consume itself, so that nothing is left of the town and what it contained nor of the thing itself'?; he would say, 'This is absurd; it is an old wives tale'. Yet this is the case with fire, although, when he heard it, someone who had no acquaintance with fire would reject it. The rejection of the strange features of the world to come usually belongs to this class. To the physicist we reply: 'You are compelled to admit that in opium there is a property which leads to freezing, although this is not consonant with nature as rationally conceived; why then is it not possible that there should be in the positive precepts of the Divine law properties leading to the healing and purifying of hearts, which are not apprehended by intellectual wisdom but are perceived only by the eye of prophecy? Indeed in various pronouncements in their writings they have actually recognized properties more surprising than these, such as the wonderful properties observed when the following figure was employed in treating cases of childbirth where delivery was difficult:—

4	9	2
3	5	7
8	1	6

IV	IX	II
III	V	VII
VIII	I	VI

The figure is inscribed on two pieces of cloth untouched by water. The woman looks at them with her eye and places them under her feet, and at once the child quickly emerges. The physicists acknowledge the possibility of that, and describe it in the book entitled *The Marvels of Properties*.

The figure consists of nine squares with a number in each, such that the sum of each row or line, vertically, horizontally and diagonally, is fifteen.

How on earth is it possible for anyone to believe that, and then not to have sufficient breadth of mind to believe that the arrangement of the formal prayers— two *rak'ahs* in the morning, four at midday and three at sunset—is so made on account of properties not apprehended by philosophical reflection? The grounds of these arrangements are the difference of the times of day , but these properties are perceived only by the light of prophecy.

It is curious, however, that, if we replace the above expressions by expressions from astrology, they admit the difference of times as reasonable. We may say, for example: 'Is it not the case that the horoscope varies according as the sun is in the ascendant in the ecliptic or in declension? And in their horoscopes do they make this variation the basis of the difference of treatment and of length of life and hour of death? Is there not a distinction between declension and the sun's being in the ecliptic, and likewise between sunset and the sun's being towards setting? Is there any way to believe this?' If it were not that he hears it in astrological terminology, he would probably have experimentally observed its falsity a hundred times. Yet he goes on habitually believing in it, so that if an astrologer says to him, 'If the sun is in the ecliptic, and star A confronts, while the ascendant is constellation B, then, should you put on a new garment at that time, you will be killed in that garment'; he will not put on the garment at that time, even though he may suffer from extreme cold and even though he hears this from an astrologer whose falsity he has acknowledged a hundred times.

How on earth when a man's mind is capable of accepting such strange statements and is compelled to acknowledge that these are properties—the knowledge of which is a miracle for some of the prophets—how does he come to reject a similar fact in respect of what he hears of the teaching of a prophet, especially when that prophet speaks truth, is accredited by miracles, and is never known to have been in error ?

If the philosopher denies the possibility of there being 160 such properties in the number of *rak'ahs*, the casting of stones (in the valley of Mina during the Pilgrimage), the number of the elements of the Pilgrimage and the other ceremonies of worship of the sacred law, he will not find, in principle, any difference between these and the properties of drugs and stars. He may say, 'I have some experience in medical and astronomical (or astrological) matters, and have found some points in the science true; as a result belief in it has become firmly settled in me and my heart has lost all inclination to shun it and look askance at it; prophecy, however, I have no experience of; how shall I know that it actually exists, even if I admit its possibility' ?

I reply: 'You do not confine yourself to believing what you have experience of, but, where you have received information about the experience of others, you accept them as authorities. Listen then to the words of the prophets, for they have had experience, they have had direct vision of the truth in respect of all that is dealt with in revelation. Walk in their way and you too will come to know something of that by direct vision'.

Moreover I say: 'Even if you have not experienced it, yet your mind judges it an absolute obligation to believe in it and follow it. Let us suppose that a man of full age and sound mind, who has never experienced illness, now falls ill; and let us suppose that he has a father who is a good man and a competent physician, of whose reputation in medicine he has been hearing as long as he can remember. His father compounds a drug for him, saying, 'This will make you better from your illness and cure your symptoms'. What judgement does his intellect make here, even if the drug is bitter and disagreeable to the taste? Does he take it'? Or does he disbelieve and say, 'I do not understand the connection of this drug with the achieving of a cure; I have had no experience of it'. You would certainly think him a fool if he did that! Similarly people of vision think you a fool when you hesitate and remain undecided'.

You may say: 'How am I to know the good will of the Prophet (peace be upon him) and his knowledge of this medical art'? I reply: 'How do you know the good will of your father, seeing this is not something perceived by the senses? The fact is that you have come to know it necessarily and indubitably by comparing his attitude at different times and observing his actions in various circumstances'.

If one considers the sayings of the Messenger of God (peace be upon him) and what is related in Tradition about his concern for showing to people the true way and about his graciousness in leading men by various acts of sympathy and kindness to improve their character and conduct and to better their mutual relations— leading them, in fine, to what is the indispensable basis of all betterment, religious and secular alike—if one considers this, one comes to the necessary knowledge that his good will towards his people is greater than that of a father towards his child.

Again, if one considers the marvellous acts manifested in his case and the wonderful mysteries declared by his mouth in the Qur'an and in the Traditions, and his predictions of events in the distant future, together with the fulfilment of these predictions, then one will know necessarily that he attained to the sphere which is beyond reason, where an eye opened in him by which the mysteries were laid bare which only the elect apprehend, the mysteries which are not apprehended by the intellect.

This is the method of reaching necessary knowledge that the Prophet (peace be upon him) is to be believed. Make the experiment, reflect on the Qur'an, read the Traditions; then you will know that by seeing for yourself.

We have now dealt with the students of philosophy in sufficient detail, discussing the question at some length in view of the great need for such criticism at the present time.

(4) As for the fourth cause of weakness of faith, namely, the evil lives of the religious leaders ('ulamā', singular 'ālim) this disease is cured by three things.

(a) The first is that you should say to yourself that the 'ālim whom you consider to eat what is prohibited has a knowledge that wine and pork and usury are prohibited and also that lying and backbiting and slander are prohibited. You yourself also know that and yet you do these latter things, not because you do not believe they are sins, but because your desire overcomes you. Now the other man's desire is like your desire; it has overcome him, just as yours has overcome you. His knowledge of other matters beyond this (such as theological arguments and the application of legal

83

principles) distinguishes him from you but does not imply any greater abstinence from specific forbidden things. Many a believer in medical science does not hold back from fruit and from cold water even though the doctor has told him to abstain from them! That does not show that they are not harmful, or that his faith in medicine is not genuine. Such a line of thought helps one to put up with the faults of the 'ulama'.

(b) The second thing is to say to the ordinary man: 'You must believe that the 'alim has regarded his knowledge as a treasure laid up for himself in the future life, imagining that it will deliver him and make intercession for him, so that consequently he is somewhat remiss in his conduct in view of the excellence of his knowledge. Now although that might be an additional point against him, yet it may also be an additional degree of honour for him, and it is certainly possible that, even if he leaves duties undone, he will be brought to safety by his knowledge. But if you, who are an ordinary man, observing him, leave duty undone, then, since you are destitute of knowledge, you will perish through your evil conduct and will have no intercessor!'

(c) The third point is the fact that the genuine 'alim does not commit a sin except by a slip, and the sins are not part of his intention at all. Genuine knowledge is that which informs us that sin is a deadly poison and that the world to come is better than this; and the man who knows that does not give up the food for what is lower than it.

This knowledge is not attained by means of the various special branches of knowledge to which most people devote their attention. As a result, most people's knowledge only makes them bolder in disobeying God most high. Genuine knowledge, however, increases a man's reverence and fear and hope; and these come between him and sins (in the strict sense) as distinct from the unintentional faults which are inseparable from man in his times of weakness. This proneness to lesser sins does not argue any weakness of faith, however. The believer, when he goes astray, repents. He is far from sinning intentionally and deliberately.

These are the points I wanted to discuss in criticism of the faults of the philosophers and the party of *ta'līm* and the faults of those who oppose them without using their methods.

We pray God Almighty that He will number us among those whom He has chosen and elected, whom He has led to the truth and guided, whom He has inspired to recollect Him and not to forget Him, whom He has preserved from the evil in themselves so that they do not prefer ought to Him, and whom He has made His own so that they serve only Him.

THE BEGINNING OF GUIDANCE

In the name of God, the Merciful and Compassionate !

The words of the Shaykh, the Imam, the learned Scholar, the Proof of Islam and the Blessing of Mankind, Abu Hāmid Muhammad ibn Muhammad ibn Muhammad al-Ghazālī aṭ-Ṭūsī—may God sanctify his rest and lighten the darkness of his tomb :

Praise be to God as is His right, and blessing and peace be upon the best of His creatures, Muhammad, and on his house and Companions after him !

With eager desire you are setting out to acquire knowledge, my friend; of yourself you are making clear how genuine is your longing and how passionate your thirst for it. Be sure that, if in your quest for knowledge your aim is to gain something for yourself and to surpass your fellows, to attract men's attention to yourself and to amass this-worldly vanities, then you are on the way to bring your religion to nothing and destroy yourself, to sell your eternal life for this present one ; your bargain is dead loss, your trading without profit. Your teacher abets you in your disobedience and is partner in your loss. He is like one who sells a sword to a highwayman, for in the words of the Prophet (God bless and preserve him), 'whoever aids and abets a sin, even by half a word, is partner with the sinner in it'.

On the other hand, if in seeking knowledge your intention and purpose between God most high and yourself is to receive guidance and not merely to acquire information, then rejoice. The angels will spread out their wings for you when you walk, and the denizens of the sea will ask pardon from God for you when you run. Above all, however, you must realize that the guidance which is the fruit of knowledge has a beginning and an ending, an outward aspect and an inward. No one can reach the ending until he has completed the beginning; no one can discover the inward aspect until he has mastered the outward.

Here, then, I give you counsel about the Beginning of Guidance. so that thereby you may test yourself and examine your heart. If you find your heart drawn towards it and your soul docile and receptive, go ahead, make for the end, launch out into the oceans of knowledge. If, on the other hand, you find that when you turn to the matter seriously, your heart tends to procrastinate and to put off actually doing anything about it, then you may be sure that the part of your soul which is drawn to seek knowledge is the evil-inclined irrational soul. It has been roused in obedience to Satan, the accursed, in order that he may lower you into the well by the rope of his deception, and by his wiles lure you to the abyss of destruction. His aim is to press his evil wares upon you in the place where good wares are sold, so that he may unite you with those 'who most lose their works, whose effort goes astray in this present life though they think they are doing well' (Q. 18, 103f.).

Moreover Satan, to impress you, rehearses the excellence of knowledge, the high rank of scholars and the Traditions about knowledge from the Prophet and others. He thus diverts your attention from sayings of the Prophet (God bless and preserve him) such as the following : 'Whoever increases in knowledge and does not increase in guidance, only increases in distance from God' ; 'the most severe punishment on the day of Resurrection is that of the scholar to whom God gave no

benefit from his knowledge' ; 'O God, I take refuge with
Thee from knowledge which does not benefit, from the
heart which does not humble itself, from the act which
is not lifted up to God, and from the prayer which is not
heard' ; 'during my night-journey[1] I passed some groups
of people whose lips were cut by fiery scissors, and I said
to them, Who are you ? and they replied, We used to
command others to do good and yet ourselves did not do
it, and to prohibit others from doing evil and yet
ourselves did it'.

Beware then, unfortunate man, of listening to his fair
words, lest he lower you into the well by the rope of his
deception.   Woe to the ignorant man, when he has not
learned even once, and woe to the learned man when he
has not put into practice what he learned a thousand
times !

People who seek knowledge are of three types. There
is the man who seeks knowledge to take it as his travel-
ling-provision for the life to come; he seeks thereby only
the Countenance of God and the mansion of eternity;
such a man is saved. Then there is the man who seeks
it for the help it gives in his transitory life in obtaining
power, influence and wealth, and at the same time is
aware of that ultimate truth and in his heart has some
perception of the worthlessness of his condition and the
vileness of his aim. Such a man is in jeopardy, for if his
appointed term comes upon him suddenly before he
repents, a bad end of life is to be feared for him and his
fate will depend upon the will (of God); yet, if he is
given grace to repent before the arrival of the appointed
term, and adds practice to theory, and makes up for the
matters he has neglected, he will join the ranks of the

[1]Muhammad's night-journey 'to the furthest mosque' (Q. 17, 1)
was developed in legend into an ascent into heaven, and even, as
here, into a descent into hell; cp. Hughes, *Dictionary of Islam*, art,
'Mi'rāj', and *Encyclopaedia of Islam*, art. 'Mi'radj'.

saved, for 'the man who repents of sin is like the man who has none'.

A third man has been overcome by Satan. He has taken his knowledge as a means to increase his wealth, the boast of his influence and to pride himself on his numerous following. By his knowledge he explores every avenue which offers a prospect of realizing what he hopes for from this world. Moreover he believes in himself that he has an important place in God's eyes because with his garb and jargon he bears the brand and stamp of the scholar despite his mad desire of this world both openly and in secret. Such men will perish, being stupid and easily deceived, for there is no hope of their repentance since they fancy that they are acting well. They are unmindful of the words of God most high, 'O ye who have believed, why do ye say what ye do not do'? (Q. 61, 2). To them may be applied the saying of the Messenger of God (God bless and preserve him), 'I fear on your account one who is not the Dajjāl (or Antichrist) more than I fear the Dajjāl', and when someone said to him, 'Who is that ?' he replied, 'An evil scholar'.

The point of this is that the aim of the Dajjāl is to lead men astray. The scholar is similar. If he turns men from this world by what he says, yet he calls them to it by what he is and what he does. A man's conduct speaks more eloquently than his words. Human nature is more inclined to share in what is done than to follow what is said. The corruption caused by the acts of this misguided man is greater than the improvement effected by his words, for the ignorant man does not venture to set his desire on this world till the scholars have done so. Thus this man's knowledge has become a cause of God's servants venturing to disobey Him. Despite that his ignorant soul remains confident ; it fills him with desire and hope, and urges him to expect a reward from God for his knowledge. It suggests to him that he is better than many of God's servants.

Be of the first group, then, O seeker of knowledge. Avoid being of the second group, for many a procrastinator is suddenly overtaken by his appointed term before repenting, and is lost. But beware, above all beware, of being in the third group and perishing utterly without any hope or expectation of salvation'.

If, then, you ask, What is the Beginning of Guidance in order that I may test my soul thereby? know that the beginning of guidance is outward piety and the end of guidance is inward piety. Only through piety is anything really achieved; only the pious are guided. Piety designates carrying out the commands of God most high and turning aside from what He prohibits, and thus has two parts. In what follows I expound to you briefly the outward aspect of the science of piety in both its parts.

5   PART I.   ACTS OF OBEDIENCE

The commands of God most high prescribe obligatory works and supererogatory works. The obligatory work is the capital on which the trading activities are based and through which man comes to safety (or salvation). The supererogatory work is the profit which gives a man a higher degree of success. The Prophet (God bless and preserve him) said: God most blessed and most high says, 'Nothing brings men near to Me like the performance of what I made obligatory for them; and through works of supererogation My servant comes ever nearer to Me until I love him, and when I have bestowed My love on him, I become his hearing with which he hears, his sight with which he sees, his tongue with which he speaks, his hand with which he grasps, and his foot with which he walks'.

You will never arrive at fulfilling the commands of God, my dear student, unless you watch over your heart and your members every single moment from morning to night. God most high is aware of your secret being; He observes your inner and your outer man; He comprehends your every glance, your every thought, your every step, and whatever else you do, moving or resting. Alike in company and in solitude you live constantly in His presence. Throughout celestial and terrestrial regions nothing is at rest and nothing moves without the Governor of the heavens and the earth being aware of it. 'He knoweth the treachery of the eyes, and what is concealed in the breasts' (Q. 40, 20); 'He knoweth the secret and what is still more hidden' (Q. 20, 6).

So, miserable man, your behaviour both inward and outward in the presence of God most high must be that of the lowly and erring slave in the presence of the powerful and victorious king. Let your endeavour be that your master may not see you where he forbade you to be and may not miss you where he commanded you to be. You will not manage to do this, however, unless you plan out your time and order your activities from morning to evening. From the moment you wake from sleep until the time when you return to your bed be diligent in performing the commands God most high lays upon you.

1. *On Waking from Sleep.*

In waking from sleep endeavour to be awake before daybreak. Let the first activity of heart and tongue be the mention of God most high. Say here: 'Praise be to God Who has made us alive after making us dead; to Him are we raised up again. It is for God that we and all creation have come to this day. His is the greatness and

6   the authority. His is the might and the power, Lord of
the worlds. In the disposition of surrender to God
(*islām*) have we come to this day, and in the word of
sincerity, in the religion of our prophet Muhammad
(God bless and preserve him) and in the community of
our father Abraham, a *ḥanīf,* [1] surrendered to God
(*muslim*), not one of the idolaters. O God we beseech
Thee that Thou wouldest direct us this day to all good.
I take refuge with Thee from committing evil this day
and from bringing evil upon a Muslim. O God, through
Thee have we come to this day, and through Thee have
we come to the night; through Thee do we live, through
Thee do we die, and to Thee are we raised up. We
beseech Thee for the good of this day and of what is in
it; we take refuge with Thee from the evil of this day and
of what is in it'.

When you put on your clothes make the intention of
fulfilling the commands of God about covering your
nakedness. Do not let your purpose in wearing clothes
be to dissemble before creatures, so that you go astray.

2.   *On Entering the Lavatory.*

When you go to the lavatory to relieve yourself,
enter with the left foot first and come out with the right
foot first. Do not take with you anything containing the
name of God or of His messenger. Do not enter bare-
headed or bare-footed. As you enter say: 'In the name
of God; I take refuge with God from filth and defilement, from soiling impurity, from Satan the accursed'.
And as you leave say: 'Have mercy on me; praise God
Who has removed from me what would harm me and
has left in me what will benefit me'. You must make
ready the pebbles (for cleansing) before relieving your-

[1] A follower of the supposed primitive and pure form of the true
religion.

self, and you must not cleanse yourself with water in the closet itself. When you pass water you must press it out and sprinkle it three times placing the left hand under the member. If you are in the desert, go away from the eyes of observers, and keep behind some object if there is one. Do not expose yourself before you reach the place where you are to sit. Do not face in the direction of prayer, and do not turn either face or back to sun or moon. Do not pass water in a place where people meet, nor in still water, nor under a tree with fruit, nor in a cave. Avoid hard ground and the windward direction so that you are not splashed, for Muhammad (God bless and preserve him) said, 'All the punishment of the tomb is from it[1].' In sitting rest upon your left foot. Do not urinate standing save in case of necessity. In cleansing yourself use both stone and water; if you want to use only one, water is preferable. When you have only stone, 7 you must use three clean dry stones, wiping the anus with them in such a way that nothing else is soiled by the ordure. Similarly wipe the penis on three places of a stone. If it is not completely cleansed after three times, make up five or seven, so that the cleansing is completed after an odd number of times. The odd is preferable; cleansing is obligatory. Cleanse yourself only with the left hand. On finishing the process of cleansing say: 'O God, purify my heart from hypocrisy, and keep my privy parts from sin'. After completing the cleansing rub your hand on the earth or on a wall, then wash it.

3. *On Ablutions.*

After you have finished thus cleansing yourself, do not omit to use the tooth-stick (*miswāk*). For that is a 'purific-ation of the mouth, pleasing to the Lord, and displeasing

[1] It was popularly believed by Muslims, though without much support in the Qur'an, that before the Last Day evil-doers suffered torment in the tomb; cp. Wensinck, *Muslim Creed*, 117-9.

to Satan'; and 'a prayer with clean teeth is better than seventy prayers without clean teeth'. The following is related from Abu Hurayrah (may God be pleased with him): 'The Messenger of God (God bless and preserve him) said, Were it not that I should distress my community, I should order them to use the tooth-stick before every prayer'. There is also the following Traditional saying of the Prophet (God bless and preserve him): 'I commanded the use of the tooth-stick until I feared it would be written down against me'.

Then sit for the ablution facing the direction of prayer in a raised place so that the splashes do not reach you. Say: 'In the name of God, the Merciful, the Compassionate. O my Lord, I take refuge with Thee from the incitements of the demons, and I take refuge with Thee, O my Lord, from their being present with me' (Q. 23, 99f.). Then wash your hands three times before placing them in the basin, and say: 'O God, I pray Thee for good fortune and blessing, and I take refuge with Thee from ill luck and disaster'.

Then make the intention of removing the filth or of fulfilling the ceremonial preparation for the Worship. The making of the intention must not be omitted before the washing of the face, for otherwise the ablution is invalid. Then take a handful of water for your mouth and rinse your mouth three times, making sure that the water reaches the back of it—unless you are fasting, in which case act gently—and say: 'O God, I am purposing to read Thy book and to have Thy name many times on my lips; through the steadfast word make me steadfast in this life and in the world to come'. Then take a handful of water for your nose, draw it in three times and blow out the moisture in your nose; while drawing it in say: 'O God, make me breathe in the fragrance of Paradise, and may I be pleasing to Thee', and while blowing it out, 'O God, I take refuge with Thee from the odours of Hell and from the evil abode'. Then take a handful for your face, and with it wash from the beginning of the flattening of the forehead to the end of the protuberance of the chin up and down, and from ear to ear across. Make the water reach the place of Taḥdhīf,[1] which is the point from which women are accustomed to remove the hair and is what lies between the top of the ear and the corner of the temples, that is, what falls from them of the forehead.

Make the water reach the four places where hair grows : the eye-brows, the moustache, the eye-lashes and the cheeks, that is, what lies in front of the ears from the beginning of the beard. The water must also reach the roots of the hair of the thin part of the beard, not of the thick part. As you wash your face say: 'O God, make my face white through Thy light on the day when Thou dost whiten the faces of Thine elect, and do not blacken my face with darkness on the day when Thou dost blacken the faces of Thine enemies'. Do not omit wetting the thick part of the beard.

Then wash your right hand, and after that the left, together with the elbow and half the upper arm; for the adornment in Paradise reaches to the places touched in ablution. As you wash your right hand say: 'O God, give me my book in my right hand and grant me an easy reckoning'.[2] As you wash your left hand say: 'O God, I take refuge with Thee from being given my book in my left hand or behind my back'. Then, moistening your hands, rub all over your head, keeping the finger-tips of right and left hands close together,

[1] A fashion of cutting the hair.

[2] At the Last Judgement, according to Islamic ideas, those who are to go to Paradise receive their book, with the account of what they have done on earth, in their right hand ; the others receive it in their left hand or from behind.

placing them on the fore part of the head and moving them back to the nape of the neck and then forward again. Do this three times—and similarly with the other parts of the body—and say: 'O God, cover me with Thy mercy, send down Thy blessing upon me, shelter me beneath the shadow of Thy throne on the day when there is no shadow save Thine; O God, make my hair and my flesh forbidden things to the Fire.'

Then rub your ears outside and inside with clean water; place your forefingers in your earholes and rub the outside of your ears with the ball of your thumbs, and say: 'O God, make me one of those who hear the word and follow the good in it; O God, make me hear the crier of Paradise along with the righteous in Paradise'. Then rub your neck, and say: 'O God, deliver my neck from the Fire; O God, I take refuge with Thee from the chains and fetters'.

Then wash your right foot and after that the left, together with the ankles. With the little finger of your left hand wash between your toes, beginning with the little toe of your right foot and finishing with the little toe of your left; approach the toes from below; and say, 'O God, establish my feet on the straight path along with the feet of Thy righteous servants'. Similarly when you wash the left, say: 'O God, I take refuge with Thee that Thou mayest not cause my feet to slip from the path into the Fire on the day when Thou causest the feet of the hypocrites and idolaters to slip'. Bring the water half way up your legs. Be careful to repeat all your actions three times.

When you have completed the ablution, raise your eyes to the heaven and say: 'I bear witness that there is no god save God alone; He has no partner; and I bear witness that Muhammad is His servant and His messenger. Glory and praise be to Thee, O God; I bear witness that there is no god save Thee. I have done evil and my soul has done wrong; I seek pardon and I turn to Thee in penitence; pardon me and repent towards me, for Thou art the Forgiving, the Merciful. O God, make me one of the penitent, make me one of the pure, make me one of Thy righteous servants, make me patient and grateful, make me to remember Thee frequently, and I shall praise Thee early and late'.

If a man says these prayers during his ablution, his sins have departed from all parts of his body, a seal has been set upon his ablution, it has been raised to beneath the throne of God and unceasingly praises and hallows God, while the reward of that ablution is recorded for him to the day of resurrection.

There are seven things to be avoided in your ablution. Do not shake your head so as to splash the water. Do not strike the water against your head and face noisily. Do not talk during the ablution. Do not repeat more than three times in washing. Do not, through mere scrupulosity, pour out more water than is necessary, for the scrupulous have a devil who plays with them, called the Walhān (lit. 'distraught'). Do not perform your ablution with water which has lain in the sun. Do not use copper vessels. These seven things are objectionable in ablutions.

There is a saying, 'If a man remembers God at his ablution, God purifies his whole body; if a man does not remember God, He purifies only those parts which the water reaches'.

4. *The Washing (or Greater Ablution).*

If you have incurred impurity from nocturnal emissions or nuptial intercourse, carry the basin to the wash-place and wash your hands first of all three times, remove any defilement from your body, and perform the 'ablution before Worship' as prescribed above, together with all the prayers, postponing only the washing of the feet so as not to make the water unusable. When you have completed the ablution, pour water over your head three times, while making the intention of removing the defilement of impurity, then over the right side of your body three times, then over your left side three times. Rub front and back of your body. Wet the hair of your head and beard. Make the water reach the bendings of the body and the roots of the hair, both thin and thick. Avoid touching your male member after the ablution; if your hand comes in contact with it, repeat the ablution.

In all of that in general the obligatory things are the intention, the removing of defilement and the comprising of the whole body in the washing. In the lesser ablution what is obligatory, besides the intention, is the washing of face and hands, including the elbows, and the washing of the feet, including the ankles, the same number of times. The exact order and everthing else are not obligatory but merely 'confirmed usages',[1] which bring much merit and an excellent reward. The man who neglects them is the loser, nay more, he endangers his actual obligations, for the additional practices (nawāfil) force one to fulfil the obligatory ones.

5. Ablutions with Sand.

You may be unable to make use of water for various reasons; there may be no water to be found although you have looked for it ; you may be excused through illness (sc. from looking for it); you may be prevented from reaching water by wild beasts or by imprisonment; the water may be required to satisfy your own or your friends' thirst; the water may be the property of some-

[1] Sunan mu'akkadah ; cp. Calverley, Worship, p. 20.

one who sells it at more than the proper price; or you may have a wound or sickness which makes you fear for your life. In one of these cases, wait until the time of the obligatory Worship comes; then look for some good ground with clean pure smooth soil; staike it with your palms and grasp it with your fingers. Make the intention of fulfilling the obligation of preparation for the Worship; rub your face with your hands, containing sand, once; you are not required to make the sand reach the roots of your hair, either thick or thin. Then taken off your signet ring, strike the sand a second time with your fingers spread out, rub your hands including the elbows with the two handfuls of sand; if you do not go over the whole area with the first handfuls, take further handfuls until you have gone over it all. Next rub one of your palms with the other, and rub the spaces between your fingers. Now perform one obligatory Worship, and any acts you please of supererogatory Worship. If you want to perform a second obligatory Worship, make a second sand-ablution from the beginning.

6. *Going to the Mosque.*

When you have completed your purification, pray in your house the two *rak'ahs* of the Dawn Worship, should the dawn have already broken. This was what the Messenger of God (God bless and preserve him) ussd to do. Then betake yourself to the mosque. Do not omit public Worship especially in the morning. Public Worship is seventeen times better than private Worship. If you are easy-going about a spiritual gaing of this kind, what benefit will you have in seeking knowledge? The fruit of knowledge is only in the activity based on it. 11

When you walk to the mosque, walk easily and calmly, and do not hurry. Say as you go: 'O God, by those who beseech Thee and by those who entreat Thee, and by this walk of mine to Thee, I swear to Thee that I set out neither lightheartedly nor heedlessly, neither from hypocrisy nor from desire to be well spoken of, but out of fear for Thy anger and longing to please Thee; I ask Thee to deliver me from the Fire and to forgive my sins, for there is none that forgiveth sins save Thee'.

7. *Entry into the Mosque.*

When you are about to enter the mosque, do so with your right foot first, and say: 'O God, bless Muhammad and the house of Muhmmad and his Companions and give them peace; O God, forgive me my sins, and open to me the gates of Thy mercy'.

Whenever you see in the mosque someone selling something, say: 'God make your trafficking unprofitable'. And when you see someone looking for a lost animal, say: 'May God not restore youre stray'—in accordance with the command of the Messenger of God (God bless and preserve him).

When you have entered the mosque, do not sit down until you have prayed the two *rak‘ahs* of 'greeting'. If you are not ceremonially pure or do not want to purify yourself, the 'other good works' [1] three times will suffice, or, according to other authorities, four times, or, according to others, three for the man who is ceremonially pure and one for the man who has made the ablution. If you have not already performed the two *rak‘ahs* of the Dawn Worship, it is meritorious to execute them instead of the 'greeting'.

When you have completed the two *rak‘ahs,* make the intention of performing a private devotion, and use the same petitions as the Messenger of God (God bless and

[1] Such phrases as 'Praise God', 'Glory be to God'; cp. al-Baydāwi on Q. 18, 44.

preserve him) did after the two *rak'ahs* of the Dawn Worship.

Say: 'O God, I beseech Thee for mercy from Thee to guide my heart, to settle my affairs, to order my disorder, to repel temptation, to reform my conduct, to preserve my secret thought, to raise up my visible act, to purify my works, to make my face white, to inspire me to walk straight, to direct me aright, to satisfy all my needs, and to keep me from all evil. O God, I beseech Thee for pure faith to fill my heart; O God, I beseech Thee for true certainty so that I may know that nothing will befall me except what Thou hast written down for me, and for glad acceptance of what Thou hast allotted to me. O God, I beseech Thee for true and certain faith which no unbelief follows; and I beseech Thee for mercy wherby I may receive the privilege of Thy regard in this world and the next. O God, I beseech Thee for patience with destiny, for salvation in the Encounter (on the Day of Judgement), and for the mansions of the martyrs and the life of the blessed, for succour against enemies and the companionship of the prophets. O God, I come to Thee in my need; my thought is weak, I fall short in my actions, I am in dire need of Thy mercy. I therefore beseech Thee, O Judge of all things, O Healer of men's breasts, that, as Thou dost rescue from the midst of the seas, Thou wouldest rescue me from the punishment of the Fire, the torment of the tombs and the imprecation of destruction, O God; and wherever my thought has been too weak, my actions too imperfect and my intention and desire too ineffective to achieve some good Thou hast promised to one of Thy servants or some good Thou givest to one of Thy creatures, I pray and beseech Thee for that, O Lord of the Worlds. O God, make us to guide and to be guided aright, not to err and lead astray, at war with

12

Thy enemies and at peace with Thy friends, loving men with Thy love and hostile with Thy hostility to those of Thy creatures who have opposed Thee. O God, this is my prayer, but it is for Thee to answer; this is my utmost endeavour, but in Thee is my trust'.

And: 'We are God's and to Him are we returning; there is no power nor might save with God, the high and mighty. O God, of the faithful covenant and wise command, I beseech Thee to protect me on the day of doom and to grant me Paradise in the day of eternity, along with the saints and martyrs who bow and prostrate themselves before Thee, and those who fulfil their covenant with Thee. Verily Thou art merciful and loving and doest what Thou wilt. Praise be to Him Who is characterized by might and holds it. Praise be to Him Who is clothed and adorned with glory. Praise be to Him Who alone is to be praised. Praise Him for His grace and favour. Praise Him for His power and goodness. Praise Him Whose knowledge encompasses all things.

O God, grant me light in my heart and light in my tomb, light in my hearing and light in my seeing, light in my hair and light in my skin, ligth in my flesh and light in my blood and light in my bones, light before me, light behind me, light to right of me, light to left of me light above me, light beneath me. O God, increase my light and give me the greatest light of all. Of Thy mercy grant me light. O Thou most merciful'.

When you have finished praying, let your occupation be only the performance of the obligatory Worship or meditation (*dhikr*) or adoration (*tasbīḥ*) or reading of the Qur'an. When, during this, you hear the call to prayer, stop what you are doing and devote yourself to making the responses to the muezzin. When the muezzin says, 'God is very great, God is very great', repeat that, and similarly with all the phrases except 'Come to Worship! come to prosperity!' after these say, 'There is no power nor might save with God, the high and mighty'. And when he says, 'Worship is better than sleep', say, 'Thou hast spoken truly and well, and I bear witness to that'. When you hear the Institution (*iqāmah*), repeat what he says, except in the case of the phrase, 'The Worship is instituted', at which say, 'God institute it and continue it as long as the heavens and the earth continue'. When you have completed the responses to the muezzin, say: 'O God, I beseech Thee **13** in the assembly of those who worship Thee and pray to Thee, at the retreat of Thy night and the advance of Thy day, that Thou wouldest give to Muhammad a place of favour and honour and an exalted degree, and raise him to the noble station Thou hast promised him, O Thou most merciful'.

If you hear the call to Worship while you are yourself engaged in Worship, complete your Worship, then catch up with the responses after the greeting in the usual manner.

When the imam commences the obligatory Worship, do nothing but follow him in it, as will be explained to you in (the chapter on) the Manner and Conduct of Worship. When you have finished say, 'O God, bless and preserve Muhammad and the house of Muhammad. O God, Thou art peace, and from Thee is peace, and to Thee peace returns. Greet us with peace, O Lord, and bring us into Thy house, the house of peace. Blessed art Thou, O Lord of majesty and honour. Praise to my Lord, the high, the most high; there is no god save God alone; He has no partner; His is the kingdom and His is the praise; He makes alive and causes to die, yet He is ever living never dying. From His hand comes all our good, and He has power over all things. There is no god save God, the beneficent, the excellent, the praiseworthy. There is no god save God, and Him alone do we worship, serving Him in sincerity, though the infidels refuse'.

Then, after that, repeat the general comprehensive prayer which the Messenger of God (God bless and preserve him) taught to 'Ā'ishah (may God be pleased with her), saying: 'O God, I beseech Thee to grant me all good things, both earlier and later, both those I know and those I do not know; I take refuge with Thee from all evil, both earlier and later, both what I know and what I do not know; I ask Thee to grant me Paradise and every word and deed, every intention and belief, that brings me near to it; I take refuge with Thee from Hell, and from every word and deed, every intention and belief, that brings me near to it. I ask Thee to grant me the good for which Thy servant and messenger, Muhammad (God bless and preserve him) asked Thee; and I take refuge with Thee from the evil from which Thy servant and messenger, Muhammad (God bless and preserve him) took refuge with Thee. O God, whatever Thou hast ordained for me, may its outcome be for my true weal'.

Then repeat the words the Messenger of God (God bless and preserve him) prescribed to Fatimah (may God be pleased with her), saying: 'O Living and Steadfast One, Lord of majesty and honour, there is no god save Thee; of Thy mercy succour me, from Thy punishment protect me, leave me not to my own care one moment; make all my life upright, as Thou didst for the righteous ones'.

Then repeat the words of Jesus (God bless and preserve both our Prophet and him): 'O God, I here this morning am unable to repel what I loathe and to gain what I hope for; by Thy hand has this morning come, not by the hand of any other; I this morning am obliged to do my work, and no needy man is in greater need than I am of Thee, while no rich man is less in need than Thou art of me. O God, let not my enemy rejoice over me, and let not my friend think evil of me; May I not come into misfortune in my religion. May this world not be the greatest of my cares nor the sum of my knowledge. Let not him who has no mercy for me prevail over me by my sin'.

Then repeat any of the well-known prayers you think fit; for this purpose learn some of those we have given in the book on 'Prayers' of *The Revival of the Religious Sciences* (*sc.* the ninth book of the first 'quarter').

Your time between the Worship and the rising of the sun should be allotted to four tasks: (a) private prayer; (b) acts of meditation and adoration, repeated with a rosary; (c) the reading of the Qur'an; (d) reflection—reflect upon your own sins, misdeeds and shortcomings in the service of your Master and how you have exposed yourself to His painful punishment and great wrath. Order your time, arranging your occupations for the whole day, so that thereby you may become aware of shortcomings that you had overlooked. Beware of exposing yourself during that day to the dire wrath of God. Make the intention of doing good towards all Muslims, and resolve that throughout the day you will occupy yourself only with obeying God most high. Go over in your heart all the different acts of obedience within your power, choose the noblest of them, and consider how to prepare the causes of it, so that you may be occupied with it. Do not omit reflection on the approach of your appointed term and the coming of death which cuts short all worldly hopes, so that matters pass from the sphere of choice, leaving only sighing and regret and long-drawn-out delusion.

Include the following ten sentences among your acts of meditation and adoration: '(1) There is no god save God alone, He is without partner, His is the kingdom and His the praise, He makes to live and causes to die, yet He is ever living never dying; from His hand comes all good, and He has power over all things; (2) there is no god save God, the King, the Truth, the Evident; (3) there is no god save God alone, the Victorious, the Lord of the heavens and the earth and what is between them, the Almighty, the Forgiving; (4) glory be to God, praise be to God, there is no god save God, God is great, there is no power nor might save with God, the High, the Mighty; (5) glorious and holy is the Lord of the angels and the spirit; (6) glory be to God, praise and glory to God the Almighty; (7) pardon me, God Almighty, save Whom there is no god, the Living, the Steadfast, I beseech Thee for repentance and pardon; (8) O God, none withholds what Thou givest and none gives what Thou withholdest, none opposes what Thou ordainest, good fortune does not benefit its possessor, apart from Thee; (9) O God, bless and preserve Muhammad and the house of Muhammad and his companions; (10) in the name of God, along with Whose name nothing harms either in earth or in heaven, He is the Hearing, the Knowing'.

Repeat each of these sentences either a hundred times or seventy times or ten times; the last is the lowest number which makes the total a hundred. Continue these acts of meditation, and do not speak before the rising of the sun. There is a Tradition (i.e., saying of Muhammad) to the effect that 'that is more excellent than freeing eight slaves of the descendants of Ishmael' (God bless and preserve both him and our Prophet); this refers to the practice of such acts until sunrise uninterrupted by conversation.

15

8. *The Time from Sunrise to Afternoon.*

When the sun has risen and is a spear's length up, perform two *rak'ahs* of the Worship, that is, at the end of the period disapproved for Worship—for Worship is disapproved between the time of the obligatory morning Worship and the time when the sun is up. Then, when the sun is high and about a quarter of the day has elapsed, perform the Forenoon Worship, four, six, or eight *rak'ahs* in pairs; all these numbers have been handed down on the authority of the Messenger of God (God bless and preserve him), with the remark that 'this Worship is the best of all; if a man wants, let him perform a large number of *rak'ahs*, and if he wants, let him perform a small number'. Between sunrise and the time when the sun begins to decline there is no religious obligation apart from these acts of Worship. The time that is left over from them you can spend in four ways.

The first and best way is to devote this time to seeking really useful knowledge as distinct from the superfluities with which people busy themselves and which they call knowledge. Really useful knowledge is that which makes you grow in the fear of God, in awareness of your own faults, and in knowledge of the service of your Lord; it decreases your desire for this world and increases your desire for the life to come; it opens your eyes to the defects in your conduct so that you guard against them ; it makes you aware of the wiles and deceptions of the devil, and how he imposes on evil intellectuals (*'ulamā'*) until he exposes them to the hate and wrath of God most high, in that they buy this world at the price of religion and make their knowledge a means of gaining wealth from the powers that be and of eating up (unjustly) the wealth of trust-endowments for the poor and orphans; all their thoughts throughout the day are directed to the quest of worldly influence

107

and a place in the hearts of men, and that forces them
to hypocrisy, to quarrelsomeness, to disputatiousness in
matters of theology and metaphysics, to boastfulness.

On the other hand, our conception of useful knowledge is what we have already expounded in *The Revival
of the Religious Sciences*. If you accept this conception,
study it and practise it, then teach it and preach it.
When a man knows these things and practises them,
16 that man shall be called great in the kingdom of
heaven, according to the witness of Jesus (peace be upon
him). [1]

When you have completed that, and have also
completed the reform of yourself outwardly and inwardly, and you still have some time free, there is no
harm in spending it in the study of the different legal
rites so as to know the less common details with regard
to the acts of service to God, and the method of media-
tion between men when the following of their passions
leads them into quarrels. That too is included in the
'non-universal duties'[2] once these important duties have
been carried out. If, however, because of its occupation
with such studies, your soul calls upon you to abandon
the acts of meditation and reading of the Qur'an
described above, you may be sure that the accursed
Devil has secretly infected your heart with a latent
disease, the love of influence and wealth. Do not let
yourself be deceived by that and become a laughing-
stock for the Devil, who will bring you to destruction
and then scoff at you. But, if you test your soul for a
time with acts of scripture-reading and devotion

---

[1] Cp. *Matthew*, 5, 19: 'whosoever shall do and teach them (*sc.*
the commandments of the law), the same shall be called great in
the kingdom of heaven'. Al-Ghazālī had read at least part of the
New Testament, and had attempted from the Gospels themselves to
refute the doctrine of the Divinity of Christ.

[2] *Furūd al-kifāyāt*; see *Encyclopaedia of Islam*, II, 61.

without through sloth finding them burdensome, and if rather it is clear that you long to attain to really useful knowledge and desire only the countenance of God most high and the mansion of the life to come, then that is better than supererogatory acts of devotion, provided the intention is sound. The important thing is soundness of intention. If the intention is not sound, it becomes the point where fools are deceived and men's feet slip.

The second way is where you are incapable of attaining to really useful knowledge but devote yourself to serving God by such activities as meditation, scripture-reading, adoration and public Worship. This is the level of those who are fervent and live a good life. By this second way also you will be successful (that is, find salvation).

The third way is to busy yourself with activities which benefit your fellow-Muslims and fill the hearts of believers with happiness, or which make it easier for good men to do good works; for example, serving the professors of God's law, and the mystics, and ministers of religion, and going about their errands; and exerting oneself in feeding the poor and unfortunate, and going about, for example, visiting the sick and escorting funerals. All that is more excellent than supererogatory acts of Worship, for these are acts of serving God which at the same time show kindness towards Muslims.

The fourth way, where you are incapable of the previous one, is to busy yourself with acquiring the necessities of life for yourself or for your family, in such a way that no Muslim suffers any harm from you nor has anything to fear from your tongue or your hand, and that your religion is upheld by your not committing any sin. If you live thus, you will reach the level of the people of God's right hand, even though you have failed to rise to the levels just described. This is the lowest level of those which are included in religion, anything below this belonging to the fields of the devils. Therefore you should busy yourself with such things, for in God is your refuge from what destroys your religion or injures one of God's servants. This (sc. destroying one's religion and harming the servants of God) is the grade of those who perish. So beware of belonging to this group.

In respect of his religion a man stands in one of three classes: (a) he may be 'safe' (or 'saved'), namely, when he confines himself to performing the duties of strict obligation and avoiding sin: or (b) he may be 'above standard' (literally, 'making a profit'), namely, when of his own will he makes an offering and performs supererogatory acts; or (c) he may be 'below standard' (literally, 'incurring a loss'), namely, when he falls short of what is incumbent upon him. If you cannot be 'above standard', at least endeavour to be 'safe', and beware, oh beware, of being 'below standard'.

In respect of other men, too, a man stands in one of three classes: (a) with regard to them he may take the place of just and generous angels, namely, by exerting himself for their ends throurh compassion and the desire to fill their hearts with gladness; or (b) with regard to other men he may occupy the position of animals and inanimate objects, namely, where they receive neither benefit nor harm from him; or (c) with regard to them he may occupy the position of scorpions, snakes and harmful beasts of prey, from which men expect no good, while fearing the evil they may cause. If you cannot reach the sphere of the angels, at least try not to fall from the level of animals and inanimate things to the ranks of the scorpions, snakes and beasts of prey. If your soul is content to come down from the highest heights, at least do not let it be content to be hurled into the lowest depths. Perhaps you will be saved by the middle way where you have neither more nor less than what suffices.

Throughout the day you must not busy yourself except with matters which will benefit you in the next life or sustain you in this, matters which are indispensable and whose aid is indispensable in the next life or in this. If in intercourse with your fellow-men, you are unable to maintain your religion (*sc*. perform your religious duties) and attain salvation, then solitude is preferable for you; so you must take to it, and find in it salvation and peace. If in solitude evil suggestions draw you away to what displeases God and you cannot subdue them by devotional practices, then you must sleep. That is the best state for you and for us all. If we are unable to gain by spoils of battle, we at least save ourselves by flight. But how mean is the state of the man who saves his religion by making his life empty! For sleep is brother of death; it is the emptying of life and assimilation to inanimate things.

9. *Preparation for the other Acts of Worship.*

You must prepare before the sun begins to decline for the Noon Worship. If you rose at night (*sc*. for prayers) or were awake for some good purpose, then take your siesta before midday; it is an aid to night-rising, just as a meal immediately before sunrise is an aid to fasting (*sc*. from sunrise to sunset). On the other hand, a siesta when you are not rising at night is like a day-break meal when you are not fasting by day. Endeavour to wake up before the sun begins to decline, perform the ablutions, go to the mosque, say the prayer of 'greeting' of the mosque, and await the muezzin and make the responses to him. Then stand up and perform the four 18

111

rak'ahs following on sun-decline. The Messenger of God (God bless and preserve him) used to protract this Worship and to say, 'at this time the gates of heaven are open, and I like to have a good work rise (*sc.* to God's throne) for me at this time'. These four *rak'ahs* before the noon Worship are a 'confirmed usage' (*sunnah mu'akkadah*). According to a Tradition, whoever performs them and makes the bowing and prostrating well, is accompanied in his Worship by seventy thousand angels, who continue to ask pardon for him until night.

Then perform the obligatory Noon Worship along with the Imam, and after that perform two *rak'ahs*, for that belongs to the fixed and established Worships. From now until late-afternoon occupy yourself only with learning or study or the succouring of a Muslim or the reading of the Qur'an, or exert yourself in procuring such necessities of life as will be of assistance to you in your religion.

Then perform four *rak'has* before the Late-afternoon Worship; that is a 'confirmed usage'. The Messenger of God (God bless and preserve him) has said, 'May God have mercy on a man who performs four *rak'ahs* before the Late-afternoon Worship'; so make an effort to receive what he (God bless and preserve him) prayed for.

After the Late-afternoon Worship let your occupations be similar to those before it. You must not be slack in the ordering of your time, doing at any moment whatever chances to present itself as it presents itself. Rather you must keep a strict reckoning with yourself and regulate your occupations and activities throughout the night and day, having something fixed to occupy every hour, and neither doing anything outside its fixed time nor doing anything else in that time. In this way the blessing on your time will be evident. If,

112

however, you are heedless and neglect yourself as the animals do, you will not know what to do each hour, so that most of your time will be used up fruitlessly and your life will have slipped from you. For your life is your capital or the basis of your trading; by it you may attain to the joy of the eternal mansion where God most high is near. Every breath you draw is a jewel of inestimable worth, which nothing can replace. Once it has passed, it cannot come back. Do not be like the poor deluded fools who delight every day at the increase of their wealth and the decrease of their days. What good is there in increase of wealth while life is decreasing? Delight only in the increase of knowledge and of good works, for these are friends who will continue to be with you in the tomb when your family and your wealth, your children and your comrades are all left behind. When the sun becomes yellow, try, before it actually sets, to return to the mosque. Busy yourself with adoration and confession of sin (literally, prayer for pardon). For this, like the period after sunrise, is an excellent time. God most high has said: 'Adore and praise your Lord before the rising of the sun and before its setting' (Q. 20, 130). Before the sun sets recite the verses: 'By the sun and his morning brightness . . . by the night when it veils him' (Q. 91, 1-4); and then the two Surahs of taking refuge (113, 114). Do not let the sun set while you are still engaged in confession.

When you hear the call to Worship, make the responses, saying after the muezzin: 'O God, at the approach of Thy night and the withdrawal of Thy day, at the assembling of Thy worshippers and the voice of Thy suppliants, I beseech Thee to grant Muhammad a place of favour and merit and an exalted degree and to raise him to the noble station which Thou hast promised

8   113

19   him, for Thou art not unfaithful to Thy promise'. And the petition as before.

Then perform the obligatory Sunset Worship, after the responses to the muezzin and the Institution. After that perform two *rak'ahs* before speaking, as that is the 'fixed arrangement' at the Sunset Worship. If you perform a further four *rak'ahs*, that is also a usage. If you are able, make the intention of remaining in the mosque in 'retreat' until nightfall, and spend the time between sunset and nightfall in Worship. Much has come to us (*sc.* in Qur'an and Traditions) about the inestimable merit of such a practice. This Worship is the *nashi'ah* or beginning of the night, since it is the first in occurrence (*cp.* Q. 73, 6). This is the Worship of the contrite. 'The Messenger of God (God bless and preserve him) was asked about the word of the Most High, They withdaw themselves from their couches (Q. 32, 18); he said, This is the Worship between sunset and nightfall; it removes all idle words of the beginning and ending of the day'.

When nightfall comes, perform four *rak'ahs* before the obligatory worship, thus filling the time between the two calls to Worship (*sc.* the call to Worship proper and the institution). There is great merit in this. A Tradition runs, 'Prayer between the call to Worship and the institution will not be unheard'.

Then perform the obligatory Evening Worship, and after it two *rak'ahs* of the 'fixed arrangement'. In the course of the latter recite the Surah of the Prostration (32), and 'Blessed is He . . . sovereignty' (Q. 25, 1-2), or Surah YS (36) and the Surah of Smoke (44). That was the practice of the Messenger of God according to Tradition. After that perform four *rak'ahs*; a Tradition indicates that this has great merit. Following on that perform the Odd Worship, three *rak'ahs* with either two salutations or one. The Messenger of God (God bless and preserve him) used to recite in these two extra Worships the Surah 'Glorify the name of thy Lord, the Most High' (87), and 'Say, O ye unbelievers' (109), and the Surah of Purity (112), and the two Surahs of Taking Refuge (113, 114).

If you have decided to be up at night for prayer, postpone the Odd Worship, so that the Odd may be your last act of Worship for the night. Then devote yourself to intellectual discourse or the reading of a book; do not give yourself up to light amusement. Let these pursuits just mentioned be your closing activities before going to sleep, for 'activities are judged by the closing ones'.[1]

10. *Going to Sleep.*

When you want to go to sleep, lay out your bed pointing to Mecca, and sleep on your right side, the side on which the corpse reclines in the tomb. Sleep is the similitude of death and waking of the resurrection. Perhaps God most high will take your spirit this night; so be prepared to meet Him by being in a condition of purity when you sleep. Have your will written and beneath your head. Repent of your faults, seek pardon, resolve not to return to your sin, and so sleep. Resolve to do good to all Muslims if God most high raises you up again. Remember that in like manner you will lie in the tomb, completely alone; only your works will be with you, only the effort you have made will be rewarded.

Do not try to induce sleep by laboriously seeing that your bed is soft and smooth; for sleep is the rejection of life, except when to be awake is unwholesome for you; in that case sleep preserves your religion. Night and

20

[1]A phrase found in Tradition referring to man's life as a whole; cp. al-Bukhārī, *Qadar*.

day are twenty-four hours; the amount of sleep you take altogether, by night or day, should not be more than eight hours. It is enough, supposing you live for sixty years, that you lose twenty of these years or a third of your life. As you go to bed make ready your tooth-stick and washing things, and resolve to get up during the night (*sc.* for prayer) or else to get up before dawn. Two *rak'ahs* in the middle of the night is one of the treasures of the righteous man. Try to multiply your treasures against the day of your poverty. The treasures of this world will be of no use to you when you are dead.

As you go to sleep say: 'In Thy name, Lord, I lay me down and in Thy name will I rise up; forgive my sins; O God, keep me from Thy punishment in the day when Thou raisest Thy servants. O God, in Thy name do I live and die; and with Thee, O God, do I take refuge from the evil wrought by evil things and from the evil of every beast Thou takest by the forelock; verily my Lord is upon a straight path (cp. Q. 11, 59). O God, Thou art the first and before Thee there is nothing; Thou art the last and after Thee there is nothing; Thou art the outmost and above Thee there is nothing; Thou art the inmost and below Thee there is nothing. O God, Thou didst create my soul, and Thou wilt bring it to death. In Thy hand is its dying and its living. If Thou makest it die, pardon it, and if Thou makest it live, preserve it from sin, as Thou preservest Thy righteous servants. O God, I beseech Thee for pardon and health. Waken me, O God, in the hour most pleasing to Thee and use me in the works most pleasing to Thee, that Thou mayest bring me ever nearer to Thyself and remove me ever farther from Thy anger. I beseech Thee and do Thou grant, I seek forgiveness and do Thou forgive, I pray to Thee and do Thou answer'.

Then repeat the Throne Verse (Q. 2, 256) and from 'The Messenger has believed' (Q. 2, 285) to the end of the Surah, the Surah of Purity (112), the two Surahs of Taking Refuge (113, 114) and the Surah 'Blessed be He in Whose hand is the kingship' (67). Let sleep come upon you while you are recollecting the name of God and are in purity. Whoever does this, lifts up his spirit to the Throne and he is written down as praying until he wakes up.

When you wake up, return to what I told you first of all, and continue in this routine for the rest of your life. If continuing thus is burdensome to you, be patient in the same way as a sick man is patient at the bitterness of sickness since he looks forward to being well again. Reflect upon the shortness of your life. If you were to live, for example to be a hundred, even that would be little compared with your residence in the mansion of the world to come, which is to all eternity. Consider how in the quest for this-world you endure hardship and humiliation for a month or a year since you hope that thereby you will have rest for twenty years, for example. How, then, do you not endure these things for a few days in the hope of having rest to all eternity?

Do not cherish long hopes which lay heavy labour upon you, but suppose that death is near and say to yourself, 'I shall endure the hardship today; perhaps I shall die tonight', and 'I shall be patient tonight; perhaps I shall die tomorrow', for death does not come upon us at a specified time or in a specified way or at a specified age; but come upon us he does, and so preparation for death is better than preparation for this world. You know that you remain here for only a brief space—perhaps there remains but a single day of your allotted span, perhaps but a single breath. Imagine this in your heart every day and impose upon yourself

21

117

patience in obeying God daily. If with the supposition that you have fifty years to live you lay upon your soul the obligation of patience in obeying God most high, your soul will break away and be difficult to handle. If you do what I suggest, you will rejoice at death unceasingly ; but if you put off and are easy-going, death will come to you when you do not reckon on it and you will sigh unceasingly. When morning comes and the night-journey is over, people praise night-travel; when death comes, you learn the outcome; 'ye shall surely know the report of it after a while' (Q. 38, 88).

We have now given you guidance in the arrangement of the periods of your day, and turn to the manner and rules of the Worship and the fast, and the rules for the leader in the Worship, for the rest of the congregation and for the Friday assembly.

11. *The Worship.*

When you have completed the purification of the body, clothing and place of Worship from all ritual and physical impurity, and have covered your privy parts from navel to knee, set your face to the Qiblah standing upright with feet apart, not touching one another.

Then recite 'Say, I take refuge with the Lord of men' (Q. 114) as a protection against the accursed Devil. Make your heart attentive, emptying it of evil suggestions. Consider in front of Whom you stand and speak, and shrink from addressing your Patron with negligent heart and breast laden with worldly suggestions and evil passions. God most high is aware of your inmost thoughts and sees your heart. God accepts your Worship only according to the measure of your humility, submissiveness, modesty and lowliness. Serve Him in your Worship as if you see Him, for, even if you do not see Him, yet He sees you.

118

If your heart is not attentive and your members not at rest, this is because of your defective knowledge of the majesty of God most high. Imagine, then, that an upright man, one of the leading members of your family is watching you to learn the quality of your Worship: at that your heart will be attentive and your members at rest. Next, turn back to your soul and say: 'O evil soul, are you not ashamed before your Creator and Patron? When you imagined that you were observed by a humble servant of His, who was able neither to benefit nor to harm you, your members were submissive and your Worship was good. Yet, though you know He observes you, you do not humble yourself before His greatness. Is He, the Most High, less in your eyes than one of His servants? How presumptuous and ignorant you are'!

Use such devices in the treatment of your heart, and perhaps it will accompany you attentively in your Worship. You are credited only with that part of your Worship which you perform intelligently. In the case of what is done negligently and inattentively you require rather to seek pardon and make atonement.

When your heart is attentive, do not omit the Institution even if you are alone ; if you expect other people to take part, make the Call to Worship, then say the Institution. When you have instituted, make the Intention, saying 'I perform for God most high the obligation of Noon Worship'. Let that be present in your heart at your *takbīr*, (*sc.* saying of *Allah akbar*, 'God is very great') and do not let the intention pass from you before you complete the *takbīr*.

At the *takbīr* raise your hands, which up till now have been hanging loosely, to the level of your shoulders. The hands should be open and the fingers stretched out, but without any effort on your part either to keep the fingers together or to keep them apart. Raise your hands to that your thumbs are opposite the lobes of your ears, the tips of your fingers opposite the tops of your ears, and your palms opposite your shoulders. When they are at rest in their place, say 'God is very great'. Then let them drop gently. In raising and dropping the hands do not push them forward nor draw them back, and do not move them sideways to right or left.

When you have dropped them, raise them afresh to your chest. Give honour to the right hand by placing it over the left. Stretch the fingers of the right hand along the left forearm so that they grasp the left wrist. Then, following the *takbīr*, say: 'Truly God is very great; His praises celebrate; magnify Him early and late'. Next recite 'I have set my face towards Him Who opened up the heavens and the earth, as a Hanīf, not one of polytheists' . . . to the end of the following verse (*i.e.* Q. 6, 70-80). Then say, 'I take refuge with God from Satan the accursed. Then recite the Fātiḥah (Q. 1) with special attention to its doubled letters,[1] trying to make a difference between your enunciation of the letters *ḍad* and *ẓā'* in your Worship. Say 'Amen', but do not make it continuous with the concluding words of the Fātiḥah. Let your recitation be audible at the Morning, Sunset and Evening Worships—that is, at the first two *rak'ahs*—unless you are following a leader. Let the 'Amen' be audible.

After the Fātiḥah at Morning Worshisp recite one from the long surahs of the division of the Qur'an called the Mufassal,[2] at the Sunset Worship one from the short surahs of that division, and at the Noon,

---

[1] I take this to refer to the assimilation of certain final letters to the initial letter of the following word ; cp. Calverley, *Worship*, p. 67.
[2] Usually from Surahs 49 to the end; cp. Calverley, *Worship*, 68n.

Afternoon and Evening Worships one from the meduim
surahs of it, as, for example, 'By the heaven decked with
constellations' (85) and those adjacent to it.

When travelling, use at the Morning Worship 'Say,
O ye unbelievers' (109) and 'Say, He is God, one' (112).
Do not go straight on from the surah to the *takbīr* of the
Bowing, but make a break between them long enough
to say 'Glory to God'. As long as you are standing keep
your eyes down and restrict your gaze to the place of
Worship (? prayer-mat); that helps to collect your
thoughts and encourages attentiveness of heart. Be
careful not to turn to right or left in your Worship.

Next say the *takbīr* of the Bowing, raise your hands as
before, and prolong the *takbīr* to the end of the Bowing.
Next place your palms on your knees, with your fingers
stretched out; make your knees straight; set your back
and neck and head all in one line; keep your elbows
away from your sides—a woman, however, does not do
this but keeps them close to her sides; and say, 'Glory to
my great Lord and praise'! If you are alone, to repeat
this up to seven or ten times is good.

Then raise your head until you are standing up- 23
right, and raise your hands while saying. 'May God
hear him who praises Him!' When you are standing
steadily, say, 'O our Lord, Thine is the praise filling the
heavens and the earth and whatever else Thou wilt'.
If you are at the obligatory Morning Worship, recite
the *Qunūt* in the second *rak'ah* when you have stood
upright after the Bowing.

Next prostrate yourself saying the *takbīr* but not
raising the hands. First place your knees on the ground,
then your hands, then your forehead, uncovered; place
your nose on the ground along with your forehead.
Keep your elbows away from your sides and your
stomach from your thighs—a woman, however, does

not do this. Place your hands on the ground oppoist your shoulders, but do not lay your forearms on th ground. Say 'Glory to my Lord, the Most High!' thre times, or, if you are alone, seven or ten times.

Then rise from the Prostration saying the *takbir* unt you are sitting upright with your left foot under yo while your right leg is erect. Place your hands on you thighs with the fingers outstretched, and say: 'Lor forgive me, have mercy on me, provide for me, guid me, restore me, preserve me, pardon me'! The prostrate yourself a second time in the same way, an sit upright to rest in every *rak'ah* not followed b Witnessing.

Next stand, placing your hands on the ground but no moving one foot forward as you rise. Begin the *takbir* c rising towards the end of the Sitting for Rest, an prolong it until you are half-way up the standin position. This Sitting should be short and as it wer snatched.

Perform the second *rak'ah* of the Worship like th first, repeating the Seeking for Refuge at the beginning At the end of the second *rak'ah* sit for the first Witnessing As you do so, place the right hand on the right thigl with the fingers closed except the forefinger and thumb which are left free. At the words 'save God', not at th words 'There is no god', point with your right forefinger Place your left hand on your left thigh with finger outstretched. In this Witnessing sit on your left foot, a between the two Prostrations. In the last Witnessing however, sit on your hip.

After the Blessing on the Prophet (God bless an preserve him) make the well-known Traditiona Supplication; during this sit on your left hip, with you left foot going out from beneath you and your right le erect. Then, when you have finished, say twice, onc

122

each side, 'Peace be upon you and the mercy of God', turning so that your neighbour may see your cheek. Make the intention of withdrawing from the Worship and the intention of peace for the angles and Muslims on either side of you. This is the form taken by the Worship of a person by himself.

The pillars of the Worship are humility and recollectedness of heart, together with the recital of the Qur'an with understanding and the making of acts of adoration with understanding. Al-Ḥasan al-Baṣrī (God most high have mercy on him) said, 'Every Worship at which the heart is not present is more likely to bring punishment than reward.' Muhammad (God bless and preserve him) said, 'A man may perform the Worship so that he is given credit for only a sixth or a tenth of it'; and 'a man receives credit only for that amount of his Worship which he understands'.

2. *Leading and Following in the Worship.*

The leader must make the Worship light, or quick, not burdensome. Anas (may God be pleased with him) said, 'Never behind anyone did I perform a Worship that was so light and yet so complete as the Worship led by the Messenger of God (God bless and preserve him).

The leader should not say the *takbir* until the muezzin has completed the Institution and until the rows of worshippers are even. At each *takbir* the leader ought to raise his voice, but those who follow him raise the voice only enough for each to hear himself. The leader makes the intention of leading in order to gain credit for this act of leading; but, even if he does not make the intention, the Worship of the congregation is still valid, provided they make the intention of following him, and they gain credit for worshipping as followers.

The leader should say secretly the Opening Supplication and the Seeking for Refuge, in the same way as
the man by himself, but he should say the Fātiḥah and
the Surah aloud on every occasion in the Morning
Worship, and in the first two (rak'ahs) of the Sunset and
Evening Worships. The individual does the same. He
(sc. the leader) says aloud the word 'Amen' in the
audible part of the Worship, and likewise the follower,
making his saying of 'Amen' coincide with that of the
leader, not come after it. The leader is silent a little at
the end of the Fātiḥah in order to recollect himself.
The follower recites the Fātiḥah audibly in this silence
so that he may be able to listen to the leader's Recital of
the Qur'an. The follower recites the Surah audibly
only if he does not hear the voice of the leader. At the
Bowing and the Prostration the leader does not say
'Glory be to God' more than three times; and at the
first Witnessing he adds nothing after the words 'O
God, bless Muhammad'. In the last two rak'ahs he
limits himself to the Fātiḥah and does not make the
Worship long for the congregation. His Supplication at
the last Witnessing is of the length of his Witnessing and
his Blessing of the Messenger of God (God bless and
preserve him).

At the Salutation the leader makes the intention of
peace for the congregation, and the congregation in
saluting makes the intention of responding to him.
After completing the Salutation the leader waits a little
and faces the people. He does not turn, however, if
there are women behind him, so that they may depart
first. No one of the congregation stands up until the
leader stands. The leader goes off either to right or
left, as he pleases, but to the right is preferable. The
leader does not specify himself (sc. say 'guide me') in the
Supplication at the Qunūt of the Morning Worship

but speaking aloud, say, 'O God, guide us', and the congregation says 'Amen'. He does not raise his hands here, since that is not established in Tradition. The follower recites the remainder of the Qunūt, consisting of the words 'Thou passest judgement, but no judgement is passed upon Thee'.

The follower does not stand alone, but enters the row of worshippers or else attracts others to himself. The follower should not precede or synchronize with the leader in his actions, but should be a little after him; he should not bend for the Bowing until the leader has come to the end of the Bowing, and he should not bend for the Prostration so long as the leader's forehead has not touched the earth.

13. *Friday*.

Friday is the festival of the believers. It is an excellent day, ordained specially for this community by God (may He be magnified and glorified). In the course of it there is a period, the exact time of which is unknown ; and if any Muslim, making request to God most high for what he needs, chances to do so in this period, God grants his request. Prepare then for it (*sc.* the Friday) on the Thursday by cleansing of the clothes, by many acts of praise and by asking forgiveness on Thursday evening, for that is an hour equal in merit to the (*sc.* unknown) hour of the Friday. Make the intention of fasting on Friday, but do so on Saturday or Thursday as well, since there is a prohibition on fasting on Friday alone.

When the morning breaks, wash, since Friday washing is obligatory on every adult, that is, it is 'established' and 'confirmed'. Then array yourself in white clothes, for these are the most pleasing to God. Use the best perfume you have. Cleanse your body thoroughly by shaving, cutting your hair and nails, using the tooth-stick, and practising other forms of cleanliness, as well as by employing fragrant perfumes. Then go early to the mosque, walking quietly and calmly. Muhammad (God bless and preserve him) has said : 'Whoever goes at the first hour, it is as if he offered a camel ; whoever goes at the second hour, it is as if he offered a cow; whoever goes at the third hour, it is as if he offered a ram; whoever goes at the fourth hour, it is as if he offered a chicken; whoever goes at the fifth hour, it is as if he offered an egg'. He said likewise : 'And when the leader comes out, the leaves are rolled up, the pens are raised, and the angels gather together at the pulpit listening to the invocation of God'. It is said that, in respect of nearness to the beholding of the face of God, people come in the order of their earliness for the Friday Observance.

When you have entered the mosque, make for the first (sc. nearest) row. If the congregation has assembled, do not step between their necks and do not pass in front of them while they are praying. Place yourself near a wall or pillar so that people do not pass in front of you. Before sitting say the prayer of 'greeting'. Best of all, however, is to perform four rak'ahs, in each of which you recite the Surah of Purity (112). There is a Tradition to the effect that whoever does that will not die until he has seen, or, in a variant reading, has been shown, his place in Paradise. Do not omit the prayer of 'greeting' even if the leader is giving the address. It is a usage to recite in four rak'ahs the Surahs of the Cattle, the Cave, TH and YS (6, 8, 20, 36) ; but, if you cannot manage these, then take the Surahs of YS, the Smoke, ALM the Worship, and the Angel (36, 44, 32, 67). Do not omit the recitation of the last Surahs on Friday evening, for in it is great merit. Whoever cannot do that

126

well, should recite the Surah of Purity (112) many times, and frequently repeat the Blessing on the Messenger of God (God bless and preserve him), especially on this day.

When the leader has come out to commence the Worship, break off your private Worship and conversation, and occupy yourself with responding to the muezzin, and then by listening to the address and taking it to heart. Do not speak at all during the address. It is related in a Tradition that 'whoever says 'Hush'! to his neighbour while the leader is giving the address, has spoken idly, and whoever speaks idly has no Friday Observance (*sc.* credited to him)'; the point is that in saying 'Hush' he was speaking, whereas he ought to have checked the other man by a sign, not by a word.

Then follow the leader in the Worship as explained above. When you have finished and said the Salutation, before speaking recite the Fātiḥah, the Surah of Purity, and the two Surahs of Seeking Refuge, each seven times. That keeps you safe from one Friday to the next, and is a protection for you against Satan.

After that say: O God, Who art rich and praiseworthy, Who createst and restorest to life, Who art merciful and loving, make me to abound in what is lawful in Thy sight, in obedience to Thee and in grace from Thee, so that I turn from what is unlawful, from disobedience and from all other than Thou'.

After the Friday Observance perform two *rak'ahs*, or else four or six in pairs. All this is traditionally related of the Messenger of God (God bless and preserve him) in various circumstances. Then remain in the mosque until the Sunset Worship or at least until the Late-afternoon Worship. Watch carefully for the 'excellent hour', for it may occur in any part of the day, and perhaps you will light upon it while making humble supplication to God. In the mosque do not go to the circles of people nor the circles of story-tellers, but to the circle of profitable knowledge, that is, the knowledge which increases your fear of God most high and decreases your desire for this world; ignorance is better for you than all knowledge which does not draw you away from this world towards the next. Take refuge with God from unprofitable knowledge. Pray much at the rising, declining and setting of the sun, at the Institution of the Worship, at the preacher's ascending of the pulpit, and at the rising of the congregation for the Worship; the likelihood is that the 'excellent hour' will be at one of these times. Endeavour on this day to give such alms as you can manage, even if it is little. Divide your time between the Worship, fasting, alms-giving, reciting the Qur'an, recollection of God, solitary devotions and 'waiting for prayer'. Let this one day of the week be specially devoted to what pertains to the future life, and perhaps it will be an atonement for the rest of the week.

14. *Fasting*.

You should not restrict yourself to fasting in Ramadan and omit the business of supererogatory works and of gaining the higher degrees in Paradise, so that you have regrets when you look at those who fast and see them in the very highest degrees, as if you were looking at a bright star far above you.

27   The excellent days—the Traditions bear witness to their excellence and honour and to the generous reward for fasting on them—are the day of 'Arafah (or 9th Dhu 'l-Hijjah) for those not making the Pilgrimage, the day of 'Āshūrā' (10th Muharram), the first ten days of the month Dhu 'l-Hijjah and the first ten of Muharram, Rajab and Sha'bān. Excellent also is the fast of the

sacred months, namely, Dhu 'l-Qa'dah, Dhu 'l-Ḥijjah, Muḥarram, Rajab; of these one is by itself and three adjoining one another. These are the days in the course of the year.

In the course of the month the days of fasting are: the first, the midmost and the last, together with the white days, namely the 13th, 14th, and 15th; in the course of the week Monday, Wednesday and Friday. The sins of the week are atoned for by fasting on Monday, Wednesday, and Friday, and the sins of the month by fasting on the first, midmost and last days of the month, and the sins of the year by fasting for the days and months mentioned.

When you fast, do not imagine that fasting is merely abstaining from food, drink and material intercourse. Muhammad (God bless and preserve him) has said: 'Many a one who fasts has nothing from his fasting save hunger and thirst'. Rather, perfect fasting consists in restraining all the members from what God most high disapproves. You must keep the eye from looking at things disapproved, the tongue from uttering what does not concern you, and the ear from listening to what God has forbidden—for the hearer shares the guilt of the speaker in cases of backbiting. Exercise the same restraint over all the members as over the stomach and genitals. A Tradition runs: 'Five things make a man break his fast, lying, backbiting, malicious gossip, the lustful glance and the false oath'. Muhammad (God bless and preserve him) said: 'Fasting is a protection; if one of you is fasting, let him avoid obscene speech, loose living and folly; and if anyone attacks him or insults him, let him say, 'I am fasting'.'

Then endeavour to break your fast with lawful food, and not to take an excessive amount, eating more than you normally eat at night because you are fasting by

9   129

day; if you take the whole amount you usually take, there is no difference between eating it at one meal at night and eating it at two meals (one by day and one by night, as when one is not fasting). The aim in fasting is to oppose your appetites and to double your capacity for works of piety. If, then, you eat food equal to what has passed from you, you have thereby made up for what has passed from you, and there is no advantage in your fast, while in addition you find your stomach oppressive. There is no vessel more hateful to God than a stomach full of lawful food. What then if what fills it is unlawful?

So when you have understood what it means to fast, do so as much as you can, for it is the foundation of devotional practices and the key of good works. The Messenger of God (God bless and preserve him) said: 'God most high said, 'Every good deed is rewarded by from ten to seven-hundred like deeds, except fasting, for that is Mine and I Myself reward it'.' Muhammad (God bless and preserve him) said: 'By Him in Whose hand is my soul, the smell of the mouth of one who fasts is found more fragrant by God than the scent of musk'. God (may He be exalted and glorified) says: 'Should one give up appetite and food and drink for My sake, then the fast is Mine, and I Myself reward it'. Muhammad (God bless and preserve him) said: 'Paradise has a gate called ar-Rayyān, the beautiful, by which none enters save those who fast'.

This is a sufficient treatment of the duties which constitute the Beginning of Guidance. If you want a discussion of Almsgiving and the Pilgrimage or a fuller treatment of the Worship and Fasting, you may consult what we have said in our work on *The Revival of the Religious Sciences*.

Religion consists of two parts, the leaving undone of what is forbidden and the performance of duties. Of these the setting aside of what is forbidden is the weightier, for the duties or acts of obedience (as described in Part I) are within the power of every one, but only the upright are able to set aside the appetites. For that reason Muhammad (may God bless and preserve him) said: 'The true Flight or Hijrah is the flight from evil, and the real Holy War or Jihād is the warfare against one's passions'.

You disobey or sin against God only through the parts of your body. Yet these are a gift to you from God and a trust committed to you. To employ God's gift in order to sin against Him is the height of ingratitude; to betray the trust which God committed to you is the height of presumption. The parts of your body are your subjects; see to it, then, how you rule over them. 'Each of you is a ruler, and each of you is responsible for those he rules over'.

All the parts of your body will bear witness against you in the courts of the resurrection, with voluble and sharp, that is, eloquent, tongue, declaring your faults before the chiefs of the creatures. God most high says (Q. 24, 24): 'On a day when their tongues and hands and feet will bear witness against them for what they have been doing'; and also (Q. 36, 65): 'Today We shall set a seal upon their mouths, and their hands will speak to Us, and their feet will testify what they have been piling up'. Then guard all your body, and especially the seven parts, for Hell has seven gates, to each of which is allotted a portion of the people of Hell.

To these gates are appointed only those who have sinned against God with these seven parts of the body, namely, the eye, the ear, the tongue, the stomach, the genitals, the hand, the foot.

The *eye* has been created for you solely in order that you may be guided by it in darkness, that you may be aided by it in respect of your needs, that by it you may behold the wonders of the realm of the earth and the heavens, and learn from the signs in them. Keep the eye from three things or four, from looking at women other than those you may lawfully look at or looking lustfully at a beautiful form, from looking at a Muslim with a contemptuous eye, from perceiving the disgrace or vice of a Muslim.

The *ear* you ought to keep from listening to heresy or slander or obscenity or vain conversation or accounts of men's wickedness. The ear was created for you solely that you might hear the word of God most high and the Traditions of the Messenger of God (God bless and preserve him) and the wisdom of His saints, and that; by gaining knowledge thereby, you might attain to the realm enduring and everlasting bliss. If you listen with your ear to anything of what is disapproved (*sc.* by God), what was for you (*sc.* in your favour) will become against you, and what would have been the cause of your success (or salvation) will be turned into the cause of your destruction. This is the greatest possible loss. Do not imagine that the sinfulness belongs only to the speaker and not to the hearer. Tradition says that 'the hearer shares (the guilt of) the speaker, and is like him a slanderer'.

The *tongue* was created for you chiefly that you might frequently engage in the mention (*dhikr*) of God most high (*sc.* in acts of adoration) and in the reciting of His book, that you might direct the creatures of God most high to His way, and that you might declare to God the

29

132

religious and secular needs of which your are conscious. If you use it for some purpose other than that for which it was created, you deny the goodness of God most high in giving it to you. It is the part of your body with most power over you and over the rest of creation. It is, above all, the slanders of the tongue which throw men into Hell on their noses. So gain the mastery over it to the utmost of your ability, lest it throw you to the bottom of Hell. There is a tradition that 'the man who speaks a word to make his friends laugh is thereby hurled into the pit of Hell for seventy years'. A Muslim met the death of a martyr in battle in the lifetime of the Messenger of God (God bless and preserve him) and someone said, 'May he enjoy Paradise', but Muhammad (God bless and preserve him) said: 'How do you know he is in Paradise? Perhaps he used to speak about what did not concern him and to be niggardly with what gained him nothing'.

With regard to your tongue there are eight things to be guarded against :

(1) *Lying.* Keep your tongue from lying, whether in earnest or in jest. Do not accustom yourself to lying in jest, for it may lead you to lying in earnest. Lying is one of the sources of the greater sins, and, if you come to be known as a liar, your uprightness becomes worthless, your word is not accepted, and (men's) eyes scorn and despise you. If you want to know the foulness of lying for yourself, consider the lying of someone else and how you shun it and despise the man who lies and regard his communication as foul. Do the same with regard to all your own vices, for you do not realize the foulness of your vices from your own case, but from someone else's. What you hold bad in another man, others will undoubtedly hold bad in you. Do not therefore be complacent about that in yourself.

133

(2) *Breaking promises*. Take care not to promise something and then fail to perform it. The good you do to people should rather be in deed without any word. If you are forced to make a promise, take care not to break it, except from inability to fulfil it or from compulsion. To do so is one of the signs of hypocrisy and wickedness. Muhammad (God bless and preserve him) said: 'There are three things, which, if a man practises secretly, he is a hypocrite, even although he fasts and performs the Worship: if, when he relates something, he lies; if, when he makes a promise, he breaks it; if, when he is given a trust, he betrays it'.

30 (30) *Backbiting*. Backbiting within Islam (*sc.* in respect of Muslims) is more serious than thirty adulteries; so it is reported in Tradition. The meaning of backbiting is the mention of matters concerning a man which he would dislike, were he to hear them; the person who does this is a backbiter and wicked, even if what he says is true. Be careful to avoid the backbiting of devout but hypocritical persons, namely, by giving people to understand something without actually stating it, as when you say, 'May God make him a better man, seeing what he has done has harmed and grieved me'; and 'Let us ask God to make both us and him better'. This combines two evil things; firstly. backbiting, for by it people come to understand; and secondly, justification of oneself and praise of oneself for freedom from sin and for goodness. Now, if your aim in saying, 'May God make him better', was to intercede for him, intercede for him in secret; if you are grieved because of him (that is, for his sake), then the sin of it is that you do not want to criticize him and make public his wickedness; but in making public your grief at his wickedness, you make a public assertion that he is wicked. Sufficient

to keep you from backbiting is the word of God most high (Q. 49, 12): 'Do not go behind each other's back; would any of you like to eat the flesh of his brother when he is dead? Ye loathe it'. Thus God compares you to one that eats carrion. How fitting that you should guard against this (sc. backbiting)!

There is another thing which will keep you from backbiting the Muslims, if you reflect about it, namely, that you should examine yourself to see whether there is any open or hidden vice in you and whether you are committing a sin, secretly or publicly. If you find that this is so in your own case, you may be sure that the other man's inability to free himself from what you attribute to him is similar to your inability, and his excuse similar to your excuse. Just as you dislike being openly criticized and having your vices mentioned, so he dislikes that. If you veil him, God will veil your faults for you; if you criticize him openly, God will give sharp tongues power over you to impair your reputation in this world, and in the world to come God will criticize you before all creatures on the day of resurrection. If, however, on examining your exterior and interior life, you do not come upon any vice or imperfection in it, either religious or secular, you may be sure that your ignorance of your vices is the worst kind of folly, and no vice is greater than folly. If God desired good for you, He would make you see your vices. To regard oneself with approval is the height of stupidity and ignorance. If, on the other hand, you are correct in your opinion, thank God for it (sc. your condition) and do not corrupt it by calumniating people and ruining their reputations, for that is the greatest of vices,

(4) *Wrangling, arguing and disputing with people about matters of theology and metaphysics.* That involves injuring

135

and disparaging the other party and showing his ignorance, and likewise involves self-praise and self-justification on the grounds of having superior intelligence and knowledge. Moreover it disturbs one's life, since when you contend with someone who is a fool he annoys you, and when you contend with an intelligent person he hates and feels rancour against you. Muhammad (God bless and preserve him) said: 'If a man avoids disputing when he is in the wrong, God builds for him a mansion in the middle part of Paradise; if a man avoids disputing when he is in the right, God builds for him a mansion in the highest part of Paradise'. The devil must not deceive you by saying to you, 'Make the truth evident, do not dissemble about it'. The devil is always trying to entice fools to evil, presented in the guise of good. Do not become a laughing-stock for the Devil and have him scoff at you. To make truth evident is good when there is someone who receives it from you, that is, by way of counsel in private, not by way of disputation. Counsel, however, has a distinctive form and character, and requires tact. Otherwise it becomes criticism, and produces more evil than good. If a man associates with the theologians (mutafaqqihah) of this age, disputation and argument come to dominate his nature, and it is difficult for him to be silent, since bad professors have suggested to people that such things constitute excellence and that what deserves praise is the power to demonstrate and debate. Flee from them as from a lion. Assuredly disputing is the cause of hatred with God and man.

(5) *Self-justification.* God most high says (Q. 53, 33): 'So do not justify yourselves, He best knoweth those who show piety'. When one of the sages (or philosophers) was asked, 'What is wicked truhfulness? he replied, 'A

136

man's praise of himself'. So beware of falling into the habit of doing that. Such conduct assuredly lowers you in people's estimation, and leads to hatred of you in God. If you want to appreciate the fact that praise of yourself does not raise you in other men's estimation, consider what happens when your acquaintances make much of their own virtue, influence and wealth. Your heart refuses to acknowledge what they claim, and your nature finds it excessive; when you have left their company, you blame them. Assuredly when you justify yourself, they likewise blame you in their hearts while you are present, and after you have left their company give tongue to their thoughts.

(6) *Cursing.* Beware of cursing anything that God most high has created, whether animal or food or man himself. Do not be categorical in bearing witness against any of the people of the Qiblah (that is, any Muslim) to the effect that he is a polytheist or infidel or hypocrite. The One Who apprehends secrets is God most high; do not interfere between God most high and His servants. On the day of resurrection you will certainly not be asked, 'Why did you not curse so and so? Why were you silent about him'? On the contrary, even if throughout your life you have never cursed Iblis and never employed your tongue in mentioning him, you will not be questioned about that or asked to give an account on the day of resurrection; but if you cursed anyone whom God created, you will have to give an account. Never blame anything that God most high created. The Prophet (God bless and preserve him) would never criticize bad food; when he wanted anything, he ate it; otherwise he left it alone.

(7) *Invoking evil on creatures.* Guard your tongue from

invoking evil on anyone whom God most high has created. Even if he has wronged you, yet the whole matter is in the hands of God most high. A Tradition says: 'Let the victim invoke evil on the wrongdoer until he requites him; if he does so, then the wrongdoer will be his creditor and he will have to give account on the day of resurrection'. A certain man said much against al-Hajjāj, whereupon one of the fathers remarked: 'As surely as God will take vengeance on al-Hajjāj for those he wronged, He will take vengeance for al-Hajjāj on those who attack him with the tongue'.

(8) *Jesting, ridiculing and scoffing at people.* Guard your tongue from that, whether in earnest or in play. It disturbs your reputation, as water in apool is disturbed by a stone, destroys respect, induces isolation (or unsociability), and harms the heart. It is the source of contumacy, anger and estrangement, and implants rancour in men's hearts. Do not associate with anyone in jesting, even if they try to associate you in their jests; do not reply to them but turn away from them until they talk about something else. Be one of those who, if they pass some idle joking, pass on with dignity.

This much about the various defects of the tongue. Nothing helps you against it except retirement and the preservation of silence wherever possible. Abu Bakr the Upright (may God be pleased with him) placed a stone in his mouth to prevent himself speaking except when necessary; he used to point to his tongue and say, 'This is what has brought all my troubles upon me'. Guard against it, for it is the chief cause of your destruction in this world and the next.

The *stomach* is to be guarded from partaking of what is unlawful or of doubtful legality. Try to obtain what is lawful, and when you have found it try to take less than your fill of it. Satiety hardens the heart (that is, makes the mind less receptive), impairs the intellect, and weakens the memory; it makes the limbs too heavy for piety and for knowledge; it strengthens the desires and aids the hosts of Satan. Satiety arising from things lawful is the source of all evil; what then of satiety from things unlawful? Likewise, to look for lawful food is a duty for every Muslim. Piety and knowledge, along with eating what is unlawful, are like building on dung. If you are content with a coarse shirt throughout the year, (or 'with one coarse shirt a year'), and two loaves of black bread in twenty-four hours, and give up delighting in the finest of delicacies, then you will never lack a sufficiency of what is lawful.

What is lawful is of many kinds. You are not required to be certain about the inner nature of things, but you must avoid what you know to be unlawful, or think to be so on the basis of some sign which is actually present and which by analogy implies unlawfulness. Now the things known to be unlawful are obvious: those thought to be so on the basis of a sign are: the property of the ruler and his deputies (or provincial governors), and the propety of those who have no means of livelihood except (professionally) mourning for the dead or selling wine or practising usury or the playing of flutes or other instruments of pleasure. The unlawful includes even the property of the man of whom you know that the major part of his wealth is quite unlawful; while it is exceptionally possible in such a case that the actual things you receive are lawful (that is, lawfully come by), yet they must be regarded as unlawful, since that is more probable (*sc.* that they are unlawfully come by). Absolutely unlawful, too, is the consuming of any trust fund where that is done otherwise than in accordance with the provision of the testator. Thus for example, what a person not engaged in theological studies receives from the trust funds of the schools is unlawful; and if a person has committed a sin invalidating his giving evidence, what he receives as a Sufi from a trust fund or other source is unlawful. We have dealt with the bases of the doubtful, the lawful and the unlawful in a special book of *The Revival of the Religious Sciences* (*sc.* Book 14). You must seek it (*sc.* the lawful), then; for to know and seek the lawful is obligatory for every Muslim, just like the five Worships.

The *genitals* should be guarded from everything which God most high has made unlawful. Be as God most high said (Q. 23, 5f.): '(Fortunate are . . .) those who their privy parts do guard, except in regard to their spouses and what their right hands possess (*sc.* slave women), for they are not to be blamed'. You will not manage, however, to guard your genitals except by guarding your eyes from looking and by guarding your heart from thinking and by guarding your stomach from what is doubtful and from satiety, for these are the movers of desire and its seed-bed.

The *hands* should be guarded from beating a Muslim, from receiving unlawful wealth, from harming any creature, from betraying a trust or deposit, from writing what may not be uttered—for the pen is one of man's two tongues, so guard it from the same things as the tongue.

The *feet* should be guarded from going to an unlawful place and from hastening to the court of a wicked ruler. To go to wicked rulers where there is no necessity nor compulsion is a grave sin, for it means humbling oneself before them and honouring them in their sinfulness, and God most high has commanded us to keep away from them when He said (Q. 11, 115): 'Lean ye not upon those who have done wrong, lest the Fire touch you . . .' to the end of the verse. If you do so, seeking their wealth, that is to hasten to what is unlawful. Muhammad (God bless and preserve him) has said: 'When a man humbles himself before an upright rich man, two thirds of his religion goes away'. That is in the case of a rich man who is upright; what then, do you think, with a rich man who is wicked?

In general, when your members move and are at rest, these acts are some of the graces of God most high to you. Do not move any of your members at all in disobedience to God most high, but employ them in obeying Him. If you fall short, the evil consequences will come back upon yourself; if you are diligent, the fruits of your activity will come back to yourself. God is rich enough to do without you and your work. It is only 'by what each one has piled up that he is held in pledge' (Q. 74, 41) (that is, men's eternal destiny depends on their conduct in this life). Beware of saying. 'God is generous and merciful; He pardons the sins of the disobedient'. This is a true word, but what is meant by it in such a context is false, and the person who repeats it is to be dubbed a fool, according to the definition of the Messenger of God (God bless and preserve him) when he said: 'The shrewed man is he who masters (or abases) himself and works for what is after death; the fool is the man who makes himself follow his passions and desires things contrary to the command of God'. If you say such a thing, you clearly resemble the man who wants to be learned in the sciences of religion but spends his time in idleness and says, 'God is generous and merciful, able to fill my heart with that knowledge with which He filled the hearts of His 34 prophets and saints, without any effort on my part, any repetition, any learning from a teacher. Again, you

141

resemble the man who wants wealth, yet does not engage in farming or commerce or any gainful occupation, but has no employment, and says, 'God is generous and merciful; 'His are the treasuries of the heavens and the earth' (Q. 63, 7); He is able to make me light upon some treasure which will make me independent of gaining a living; He has in fact done that for some men'.

Now you, on hearing what these two men say, count them fools and scoff at them, even although their description of the power and generosity of God most high are true and correct. In exactly the same way men of insight in religion laugh at you when you try to obtain forgiveness without making any effort for it. God most high says (Q. 53, 40): '(Has he been told) that man gets exactly the result of his striving'? and again (Q. 52, 16): 'ye are only being recompensed for what ye have been doing'; and again (Q. 82, 13f.): 'verily the virtuous are in delight, and verily the scoundrels are in a hot place'. So, if you do not, in reliance on His generosity, give up all effort to get knowledge and wealth, likewise do not give up making provision for the world to come and do not become remiss. The Lord of this world and of the next is one, and in both He is generous and merciful; His generosity does not increase through your obedience, but it consists in His making easy for you the way by which you arrive at the enduring and eternal realm through patience in setting desires aside for a few days. Such is His great generosity. Do not repeat to yourself these stupidities of the idlers, but imitate men of prudence and resolution, the prophets and the righteous. Do not long to reap what you did not sow. Would that all who fasted and performed the Worship and engaged in the Holy War and were pious had been forgiven!

These are all the things from which you must guard your external members. The acts of these members develop only through the attributes of the heart. If, then, you want to guard your members, you must purify your heart, that is, be inwardly pious and not merely outwardly. The heart is the 'morsel of flesh. (Q. 22, 5; 23, 14; sc. second stage of the embryo) whose soundness leads to the soundness of the whole body; so see to its soundness in order that thereby your members may be sound.

THE SINS OF THE HEART

The blameworthy qualities in the heart are many, the purification of the heart from its vices is lengthy, and the means of treating these is obscure. People are so lacking in concern for themselves and so occupied with the vain pomp of the world that the knowledge and practice of that treatment have altogether disappeared. We have dealt fully with all that in our work on *The Revival of the Religious Sciences*, in the parts about Things Destructive and Things Salutary, (the third and fourth 'quarters'); but here we warn you against three of the evil dispositions of the heart—the most prominent among the religious scholars of our time—so that you may be on your guard against them; for they are both destructive 35 in themselves and the roots of all other evil dispositions. They are envy, hypocrisy and pride (or self-admiration). Endeavour to purify your heart from them. If you master these, you know how to guard against the others mentioned among the things destructive ; if you are unable to deal with them, you will be all the more unable to deal with others. Do not imagine that you will preserve a sound intention in your pursuit of learning while there is any envy, hypocrisy or pride in your heart.

143

Muhammad (God bless and preserve him) said: 'Three things are destructive, sordid avarice, desires given rein to, and admiration of oneself'.

Envy. This is a form of avarice, for the miser is the man who is niggardly towards others with his possessions; the grudging person is the one who is niggardly towards the servants of God most high with the favour of God where that is in the treasuries of His might and not in his own treasuries—so his avarice is greater. The envious man is the one who is pained when God most high out of the treasuries of His might bestows on one of His servants knowledge or wealth or popularity or some piece of good fortune, and who therefore wants that favour taken away from the other person, even though he himself will not obtain any advantage from its removal. This is the depths of evil.

Hence the Messenger of God (God bless and preserve him) said : 'Envy eats up good deeds as fire eats up wood'. The envious man suffers punishment and receives no mercy. He is continually suffering punishment in this world, for the world never lacks among his contemporaries and acquaintances many on whom God has bestowed knowledge or wealth or influence, and thus he continually suffers punishment in this world until his death. And the punishment of the world to come is even greater and more severe. Indeed a man does not arrive at true faith so long as he does not want for the rest of the Muslims what he wants for himself. Indeed, he must be equal to them in weal and woe. The Muslims are like a single building, one part of which supports the other; they are like a single body, in which, if one member suffers, the rest of the body is affected. If you do not find this state of affairs in your heart, then it is more important for you to busy yourself with seeking deliverance from destruction than to busy

144

yourself with recondite questions of casuistry and the science of litigation.

Hypocrisy. This is latent polytheism, one of the two forms of polytheism. It consists in your quest for such a place in the hearts of people that you thereby obtain influence and respect. The love of influence is one of the 'desires given rein to', and through it many people go to destruction. Yet people are destroyed only by themselves. If people really judged objectively, they would realize that it is only people's hypocrisy which is the motive of most of their intellectual pursuits and acts of Worship, not to mention their customary activities; and his hypocrisy renders their acts of no avail. Thus we find in Tradition, 'On the day of resurrection orders will be given to take the martyr to the Fire, and he will say, "O Lord, I was martyred fighting in Thy path", and God most high will say to him, "You wanted it to be said that so and so is brave; that has been said, and that is your reward".' The same will be said of the scholar, the man who has performed the pilgrimage to Mecca, and the reciter of the Qur'an. 36

Pride, arrogance, boastfulness. This is the chronic disease. It is man's consideration of himself with the eye of self-glorification and self-importance and his consideration of others with the eye of contempt. The result as regards the tongue is that he says, 'I . . I . .'; as accursed Iblis said (Q. 38, 77): 'I am better than he; Thou hast created me of fire, but him Thou hast created of clay'. The fruit of it in society is self-exaltation and self-advancement and the endeavour to be foremost in discussion and resentment when what one says is contradicted. The arrogant man is he who, when he gives advice, mortifies, but, when he receives it, is rude.

Every one who considers himself better than one of the creatures of God most high is arrogant. Indeed, you ought to realize that the good man is he who is good in God's sight in the mansion of eternity; and that is something unknown to man, postponed to the End. Your belief that you are better than others is sheer ignorance. Rather you ought not to look at anyone without considering that he is better than you and superior to you. Thus, if you see a child, you say, 'This person has never sinned against God, but I have sinned, and so he is better than I'; and if you see an older person, you say, 'This man was a servant of God before me, and is certainly better than I'; if he is a scholar, you say, 'This man has been given what I have not been given and reached what I did not reach, and knows what I am ignorant of; then how shall I be like 'him'? and if he is ignorant, you say, 'This man has sinned against God in ignorance, and I have sinned against him knowingly, so God's case against me is stronger, and I do not know what end He will give to me and what end to him'; if he is an infidel, you say, 'I do not know; perhaps he will become a Muslim and his life will end in doing good, and because of his acceptance of Islam something of his sins will be taken away, as a hair is taken from dough; but as for me—God is our refuge (*sc.* God grant it does not happen)—perhaps God will lead me astray so that I become in infidel and my life ends in doing evil, and then tomorrow he will be among those brought near to God and I shall be among the punished'.

Arrogance will not leave your heart except when you know that the great man is he who is great in the sight of God most high. That is something which cannot be known until the end of life, and there is doubt about that (*sc.* the end and whether it will be good or bad). So let fear of the end occupy you and keep you from making yourself out, despite the doubt about your end, to be above the servants of God most high. Your certitude and faith at present do not exclude the possibility of your changing in the future; for God is the disposer of hearts; He guides whom He will and leads astray whom He will.

The Traditions about envy, arrogance, hypocrisy and pride are numerous. A single comprehensive Tradition about them will suffice you. Ibn al-Mubārak related, with a chain of authorities going back to a certain man, that this man said to Mu'ādh, 'O Mu'ādh, tell me a Tradition you heard from the Messenger of God (God bless and preserve him).' The man continued : 'Mu'ādh wept until I thought he would never cease, but at length he ceased; then he said: 'I heard the Messenger of God (God bless and preserve him) saying to me: 'I am going to tell you a Tradition (or tell you of a happening), Mu'ādh ; if you remember it, it will benefit you before God, but if you forget it and do not remember it, your plea of defence before God on the day of resurrection will be removed. O Mu'ādh, God (may He be blessed and exalted) before creating the heavens and the earth created seven angels, and to each of the heavens He appointed one of these seven angels as keeper. Now the guardian angels are ascending with man's work from morning to evening; and the work has a light like the light of the sun. When they bring it up to the lowest heaven, they increase and multiply it, and the angel at the gate says to the guardians. 'With this work strike the face of the doer of it; I am in charge of backbiting ; my Lord has commanded me not to allow the work of anyone guilty of backbiting to pass beyond me.'' He continued: 'Then the guardians bring one of man's good works and increase and multiply it, until they reach the second heaven with it. The angel responsible for it says, 'Stand and with this work strike the face of the worker of it, for in his work he sought worldly honour ; my Lord has commanded me not to allow his work to pass beyond me; he boasted in men's society of his superiority; I am the angel dealing with boastfulness.'' He continued : 'The guardians ascend with a man's work, so bright with light from alms and Worship and fasting that the guardians were astonished. They passed with it to the third heaven, and there the angel in charge says to them, 'Stand and with this work strike the face of the worker of it; I am the angel dealing with arrogance; my Lord has commanded me not to let his work pass beyond me for he has treated people arrogantly in society.'' He continued : 'The guardians ascend with a man's work shining brightly like a star and ringing from the acts of adoration and Worship, from fasting and from the greater and lesser pilgrimages, and they pass with it to the fourth heaven. Then the angel responsible for that says to them, 'Stand and with this work strike the face and back and front of the doer of this work I am in charge of pride ; my Lord has commanded me not to let this act pass beyond me ; whenever this man performed any work pride entered into it.'' He continued: 'The guardians ascend with a man's work and pass with it to the fifth heaven; it is like a bride being conducted to her husband. The angel responsible for it says to the guardians, 'Stand and with this work strike the face of the doer of it, and carry him away and place him on his shoulder; I am the angel dealing with envy ; this man used to envy whoever studied and performed a work like his and all who were superior to men in some way; he used to envy them and slander them ; my Lord has commanded me not to allow his work to pass beyond me.'' He continued : 'The guardians ascend with a man's work, radiant as

38

148

the moon from Worship and almsgiving and the greater and lesser pilgrimages and the holy war and fasting, and they pass with it to the sixth heaven, where the angel responsible for that says to them, 'Stand and with this work strike the face of the doer of it; he never had mercy on any of God's servants who had met with misfortune or sickness, but rejoiced at that; I am the angel of mercy; my Lord commanded me not to allow his work to pass beyond me.'' He continued: 'The guardians ascend with a man's work consisting of Worship and fasting and the spending of money (in good causes, or otherwise as alms) and the holy war and continence; it had a sound like that of bees and a radiance like that of the sun; along with it were three thousand angels and they passed with it to the seventh heaven. The angel responsible for that said to them, 'Stand and with that work strike the face of the doer of it and with it strike his limbs and lock up his heart; I veil from my Lord every work that is not done for the sake of my Lord; this work was done for the sake of something other than God most high; he did it for the sake of honour among the religious scholars ('ulamā) and fame among the intellectuals and renown among the cities; my Lord commanded me not to allow his work to pass beyond me; every work not done purely for God is hypocrisy, and God does not receive the work of the hypocrite.'' He continued: 'The guardians ascend with a man's work consisting of Worship, almsgiving, fasting, the greater and lesser pilgrimages, a good character, observance of silence and recollection of God most high. It is accompanied by the angels of the seven heavens until they have passed through all the veils to the presence of God most high. Then they stand before Him and bear witness to Him of the good work, performed solely for the sake of God most high;

149

and God most high says, "You are the guardians over the work of My servant, but I am the Watcher over his heart; this act was not done for My sake, but for the sake of something else; so My curse is upon him." Then the angels all say, "Thy curse and our curse be upon him"; and the seven heavens and those in them curse him." ' At that Mu'ādh wept, and then continued: "I said: 'O Messenger of God, you are the Messenger of God, and I am Mu'ādh; how shall I have purity of intention and salvation'? Muhammad said: 'Imitate me, even if you fall short somewhat in what you do. O Mu'ādh, guard your tongue from slandering your brothers who know the Qur'an by heart; attribute your sins to yourself and not to them; do not justify yourself and blame them; do not exalt yourself above them; do not mingle the work of this world with the work of the world to come; do not act arrogantly in society so that men avoid you because of your bad character; do not whisper to one man while another is also present; do not magnify your importance above other men so that you lose the good things of both this world and the world to come ; do not tear to pieces people's characters so that on the day of Resurrection the dogs of Hell tear you to pieces in Hell. God most high says (Q. 79, 2); "By those who draw forth"; do you know what these are, O Mu'ādh?' I said: 'What are they, O Messenger of God (may you be ransomed by my father and mother)?' He said: 'The dogs in Hell drawing the flesh from the bones'. I said: 'O Messenger of God (may you be ransomed by my father and mother) who is able to acquire these good qualities, and who will escape from these dogs?' He said: 'O Mu'ādh, it is indeed easy for him for whom God makes it easy.' "

Khālid b. Mi'dān said: 'I never saw anyone more

assiduous in reading the noble Qur'an than Mu'ādh on account of this noble Tradition'.

So, you who desire knowledge, reflect on these (sc. bad) qualities. Undoubtedly the greatest cause of these vices becoming established in the heart is the pursuit of knowledge in order to dispute with others and outshine them. The ordinary man is far removed from these bad qualities, but the scholar or theologian is in the way of them and is exposed to destruction because of them. Consider, then, which of your affairs is most important —to learn how to guard against these 'things destructive' and to occupy yourself with the improvement of your heart and the preparation of your eternal life— or whether it is more important to engage along with the others in the pursuit of such knowledge as will increase your arrogance, hypocrisy, envy and pride, until along with the others you perish.

Undoubtedly, these three qualities are the roots of the vices of the heart, and they have a single field of operation, namely, the love of this world. For that reason the Messenger of God (God bless and preserve him) said, 'The love of this world is the fount of all sin'. At the same time, this world is a field sown for (reaping in) the world to come. If a man takes from this world only as much as is necessary, to help him with regard to the world to come, then this world is for him a field that has been sown; but if he wants this world to enjoy it, then this world is his ruination.

The above is a small part of the science of piety in its exterior aspects and it is the Beginning of Guidance. If you try it out on yourself in practice and find it acceptable to you, then you must turn to *The Revival of the Religious Sciences* and become acquainted with piety in its interior aspect. When you have built up the interior of your heart in piety, at that the veils between you and your Lord will be removed, the light of mystic knowledge will be revealed to you, there will burst forth from your heart the springs of wisdom, and the secrets of the supernal realm will be made clear to you. Such sciences will become familiar to you that you will hold of no account these new-fangled sciences of which there was no whisper in the days of the Companions (may God be pleased with them) and the Followers. If, however, you pursue the science of argument and counter-argument, of contradiction and dispute, how great will be your misfortune, how protracted your toil, how great your disappointment and your loss! Do what you will. This world, to the pursuit of which you make your religion a means, will nevertheless not be vouchsafed to you, and the world to come will be kept from you. The man who makes his religion a means to the gaining of this world, will lose both worlds alike ; whereas the man who gives up this world for the sake of religion, will gain both worlds alike.

40   This is all the Guidance to the Beginning of the way in respect of your dealings with God most high by performing what He commands and avoiding what He forbids.

(The remainder of the book as it now stands is probably not authentic.)

INDEX

Ablutions, 93-9, 111; *see also* Washing.

Abraham, 59, 92.

Abū Bakr, 138.

Abū Yazīd al-Bistāmī, 54.

Abū Hanīfah, 48.

Abū Hurayrah, 94.

Abū Tālib al-Makkī, 54.

Ahl al-Haqq, 44.

Ahl al-Ibāhah, (Latitudinarians), 72, 77.

Ahmad b. Hanbal, 44-5.

'Ā'ishah, 104.

'Alī, 39, 40.

Alms, 47.

Anas (b. Mālik), 123.

Antichrist, 89.

'aql, 64, 66, 70.

Aristotle, 13, 32, 37, 53.

al-Ash'arī, 13.

Astronomy, astrology, 65-6, 77, 80-1.

Authoritative Instruction, *see* ta'līm.

Authority, *see* taqlīd.

Backbiting, 129, 134-5, 147.

Baghdād, 11, 19, 52, 56, 58-9, 76.

Bātinīyah, 13, 20, 26-7, 52 ; *see also* Ta'līmīyah.

al-Baydāwī, 100n.

Blessing on the Prophet, 122, 124.

Bowing, *see* rukū'.

Breaking promises, 134.

Brethren of Purity, 41-2, 53.

al-Bukhārī, 115n.

Call to Worship, *see* Muezzin.

Calverley, E. E., 15n., 61n., 98n., 120n.

Chemistry of Happiness (*Kimiyā' as-Sa'ādah*), 77.

Christian, 21, 39.

Cursing, 137.

Dahrīyūn, 30-2.

ad-Dajjāl (Antichrist), 89.

Damascus, 59.

Decisive Criterion (*Faysal at-Tafriqah*), 38.

dhawq (immediate experience), 54, 62, 66, 68.

dhikr, 102, 105, 108, 132.

Dreams, dream-states, 64, 66.

Ear, 132.

Ecstasy, 54, 60, 62.

EI (*Encyclopaedia of Islam*), 21n.

Envy, 145-5.

Ethics, 33, 38-9.

Eye, 132, 140.

Faith, *see* imān.

fanā' (absorption), 61.

al-Fārābī, 32, 37, 72.

Fasting, 111, 125, 128-30, 134, 149.

Fātihah (first sūrah of Qur'ān), 120, 123, 127.

Fātimah, 104.

Feet, 140-1.

fitrah, 21n.

Food of the Hearts (*Qūt al-Qulūb*), 54.

Fundamental Difference (*Mufassal al-Khilāf*), 52.

furūd al-kifāyāt, 108.

Galen, 67.

Genitals, 140.

al-Ghazālī, 11-15.

Gospels, 108n.